Tomorrow's Textbook

Tomorrow's Textbook

VICTOR MOLLO

METHUEN

First published in Great Britain 1985
by Methuen London Ltd
11 New Fetter Lane, London EC4P 4EE
Copyright © 1985 Victor Mollo

Typeset by Words & Pictures Ltd
Thornton Heath, Surrey
Printed in Great Britain by
Redwood Burn Ltd., Trowbridge, Wiltshire.

British Library Cataloguing in Publication Data

Mollo, Victor
 Tomorrow's textbook.
 1. Contract bridge
 I. Title
 795.41'5   GV1282.3

 ISBN 0-413-59130-1
 ISBN 0-413-59330-3 Pbk

Contents

A Look at Tomorrow

With perfection through precision as the goal, science has been the main source of inspiration for bridge thinkers during the past twenty years or more. In the process, practice has all too often been subordinated to theory.

There's not much further to go along this road. In bidding as in play, technique can always be improved, but beyond a certain point the reward is no longer commensurate with the effort. Logical deduction, the ability to draw inferences, a sense of anticipation, that is the target area for tomorrow, and these are the themes of *Tomorrow's Textbook*.

The play shapes the bidding

We need a new approach. No longer should bidding and card-play be treated as separate subjects, each claiming a series of chapters to itself, as in standard textbooks. They are two sides of the same coin. Neither is valid without the other and no chapter is complete without both.

As Hamlet might have said, a contract is neither good nor bad but playing makes it so. Only when you have put your bidding through the crucible of card-play can you judge its merits. Only when you have seen how tricks are made can you gauge how many you should contract for.

In the pages that follow you will be asked 230 questions — first on how you would bid, then on how you would play the same hands. You will then see not only which bids and plays were right or wrong, but above all what made them so.

Systems and cyphers

Systems will be conspicuous by their absence. The less of them the better, I say, but in themselves they don't much matter. Good bridge is based on reason, not on rules. Taboos and sacred cows have no place in it. For the sake of simplicity, and that's a top priority, all our bids will be natural in so far as possible. We shall not be playing 5-card majors or weak two-bids, though that is something the reader will hardly notice. And since both are popular, we shall alternate between the weak no-trump (12-14) and the strong (15-17), testing each in turn in different situations.

Some conventions have gained such wide acceptance that they must be treated with respect and the 'Overture' will introduce most of them. But the question arises: what is a convention?

Because there are only thirty-eight words in the bidding vocabulary certain messages must be compressed, so an artificial bid replaces two or more natural ones. There is, however, a price to pay. If 2♣ is used to describe a game hand or to enquire if partner has a 4-card major, the bid can no longer be used in its natural sense. This is not much of a sacrifice in the case of 2♣ because in its own right it is of little value as a bid. Blackwood falls into a different category in as much as 4NT can be used as a natural, quantitative bid in some situations, without impairing its principal function as an ace-locating device in others. In short, you can have your cake and eat it too. But there's still a price to pay. Blackwood is so simple that the temptation to abuse it is to many players almost irresistible and, used indiscriminately, there's more to lose on the swings than there is to gain on the roundabout. I shall be warning you of the pitfalls as we go along.

The proliferation of artificial bids and gadgets of every sort is due almost entirely to the popularity of duplicate. Regular partnerships, with plenty of opportunities for practice and discussion, can afford to adopt a code and inflict it on others in return for a similar disservice.

At rubber bridge, with frequent changes of partner, only a few of the most popular conventions are permitted. At the St James's Bridge Club in London, where some of Britain's best players foregather daily, Stayman, Blackwood and the Unusual No-Trump are the only ones in regular use, and though shocking contracts are not unknown, few good ones are missed through lack of the machinery to reach them. I have yet to hear an expert complain. And what a joy it is for all to speak the same language and to get on with the game!

Beware of placebos

The price of conventions goes beyond taking natural bids out of circulation. Gadgets are not innocuous placebos which may do little good but cause no harm. They distort and distract. Instead of thinking out the next move and planning others to follow a player uses a formula, a thought-substitute.

This brings me to the point-count, the greatest thought-substitute of all. Of course I do not deny the Milton Work Scale a place of honour in its proper context, any more than I oppose the intelligent use of conventions. It's the substitution of the count and of codes for the little grey cells that I deplore.

Instead of assessing and reassessing his hand in the light of the bidding, the lazy player — and how many are not? — applies a ready-made measure. Two doubleton queens in opponents' suits, a source of weakness, are rated at 4 points — the same as the ace of trumps! A singleton, flanked by five prospective trumps, is quoted at 3, whether partner, who opened 1NT, is likely to have three cards in the suit or a singleton, opponents having shown ten or eleven between them. For the points merchant, duplication of values doesn't exist.

On paper all points are equal. At the table some are more equal than others.

Count points, theirs, not yours

We shall continue to count points in the bidding tomorrow — in moderation — but above all we shall make good use of them in the play, for that is where they are most helpful. Let us take a clear-cut example.

A player, who passes as dealer, shows up with an A K and an ace, 11 points. You know he cannot have another king and, the finesse being doomed, you pin your hopes on dropping his partner's bare king. When it happens, as it does on occasion, the kibitzers gasp. East, who opened 3♡, follows three times in spades and four times in clubs. You finesse the ◇8 and, needless to say, it wins. The kibitzers gasp again.

Magic? If so, all you need to be a magician is to count the cards and the points — theirs, not yours. Sometimes it doesn't matter and at others it is invaluable, so do it all the time. Think of the believer who was trying to convert the sceptic.

"Suppose," said the believer, "that a man climbed to the top of the Eiffel Tower, jumped and landed safely. Wouldn't that be a miracle?"

"No," replied the sceptic. "If such an extraordinary thing happened, it would mean that the man's fall had been broken by some freak gusts of wind or some other natural phenomenon."

"Suppose," went on the believer, "that the same thing happened to the same man a second time?"

The sceptic shook his head.

"A third, a fourth and a fifth time," persisted the believer. "Surely it would be a miracle."

3

"Oh, by that time it would have become a habit," retorted the sceptic.

And that is precisely what counting opponents' points and reading their cards should be — a habit. Acquired at an early stage in a player's education, it will come naturally and require no effort later.

Teaching habits

It is easier, much easier, to teach people to play well than not to play badly. Many textbooks, including mine, explain in detail, with a wealth of examples, the mechanics of squeezes, end-plays, trump coups and dummy reversals, and of course there are chapters on card-reading. But how do you instil the habit? Can a textbook do it at all?

The proof of the pudding is in the eating. It is through textbooks that players have come to apply the rule of two and three to sacrifices, to be guided in the choice of plays by percentage tables and, more especially of course, to count points in and out of season. All these are habits. Good habits can be similarly inculcated to correct the flaws in others.

Once more, let us take a concrete example. Until fairly recently squeeze play was regarded as the prerogative of the expert. It is so no longer. The subject has been discussed so often in books and articles that even a double squeeze no longer mystifies the average player. Yesterday's textbooks have done their work well and the readers are ready for tomorrow's. They are familiar with the terminology — menace, squeeze card, rectifying the count. The usual diagram of the three- or four-card ending presents no problem. Discarding before dummy, West, with guards in two suits, must relinquish one of them — he has been squeezed.

That's easy. The difficult part is to visualise the end-position at the beginning when so many other cards obscure the view. There are times when an expert can see from the start that only a squeeze will bring the contract home. More often the need for it, and indeed the possibility, is not apparent till later — too late to prepare the ground. The expert bears this in mind and often concedes a trick early on to rectify the count, *in case* the need arises. That again is a habit — playing the hand in such a way that as many options as possible are kept open.

What is true of squeezes is no less true of end-plays, trump-reducing plays and other manoeuvres. The execution is a matter of technique. The application is an attitude of mind, a habit of looking for extra chances should others fail.

Similarly, safety plays can be learned and memorised, but the awareness that they may be needed is, or rather should be, a habit — the habit of guarding against misfortune.

The technique, the mechanics, will be the same tomorrow as they are today, but the emphasis will be less on the apparatus itself and more on anticipating the occasions for its use.

Grey areas

Another subject for tomorrow is the treatment of 'grey areas'. In a textbook a bid is right or wrong. This or that is the correct card to play. Such may often be the case, but it isn't *always* the case, which is why experts on the panels of bridge magazines — the juries as they are called in France — so often disagree. Between right and wrong there may be a grey area. No textbook can put an end to uncertainty, but what it can do is to indicate the factors which should tilt the balance one way or the other. If there isn't always a right view, there are snares and delusions which can induce the wrong one. Against these the reader can be warned. Intelligent speculation is very much a part of bridge.

A good word for the result merchant

Tactics and psychology are important at every stage and become increasingly so once the elements of technique have been mastered. The wrong bid or play on Monday may be the right one on Tuesday. You may have a different partner or different opponents, and though in theory no hand should be influenced by those which have preceded it, this isn't always so in practice. In a match, as in money bridge, players may take risks to make up for a bad result — or hang back after incurring a penalty. A winning vein, an unlucky streak, all can make a difference. So spare a thought for the result merchant. He is often right, though he rarely knows why.

The end and the means

I firmly believe that a surfeit of sophistication is counter-productive, that simple, natural methods impose less strain, give greater pleasure and are, in the long run, more rewarding. But whatever your philosophy and whichever methods you pursue, never sacrifice the end to the means. The end of course is, and always must be, to get the best possible result from your cards. And that is the motif of *Tomorrow's Textbook*.

Overture

The first fifteen hands outline the main themes which run through the hundred that follow. In bidding they highlight the treatment — and the ill-treatment — of widely accepted conventions, and the different usages of the opening no-trump, weak and strong. In the play, overleaf, the reader is invited to set in motion the wheels of every mechanism in turn. The manoeuvres available to declarer are strictly limited, in contrast with the countless situations which condition their execution. Should the reader be puzzled later by some facet of squeeze play, trump reduction or throw-in — or by some inferential cue-bid or forcing pass — he may find it helpful to turn back to its counterpart in the 'Overture' and put every piece of the apparatus under the spotlight. Unencumbered by extraneous factors, the essentials will be easier to grasp.

Many a problem arises because it is so hard to see the wood for the trees. The purpose of the 'Overture' is to get the trees out of the way — before reaching the forest.

1

	♠ 6 5 3		♠ A 10 9
	♡ A 3 2	**N**	♡ K 10 7
Dlr. West	◇ Q J 2	**W E**	◇ A 10 9 3
Both Vul.	♣ A K 4 2	**S**	♣ 8 7 5

West	*North*	*East*
1NT (12/14)	Pass	?

The opening 1NT is the best bid of all, conveying in one go a picture of shape and strength within narrow limits. Partner knows at once which side holds the balance of power. Opponents don't, and if they come in, they must do it at the two level.

Because of these advantages — and of its greater frequency — many players prefer a weak no-trump (12-14) to the strong (15-17), regardless of vulnerability. Others, especially in Britain, like a variable no-trump, strong vulnerable, weak non-vulnerable.

To whichever school you belong — weak, strong or variable — it is important to grasp the key features of the weak no-trump. Its Achilles' heel is the penalty to which it is liable when opponents double and partner has nothing and no escape suit. The other side of the medal is the dilemma confronting opponents. Should they step in, risking a penalty, or should they keep quiet when they have perhaps a partial or even a game? This happens often and to put maximum pressure on the enemy, partner passes on fair hands, unless he sees prospects of game. To give nothing away he rarely bids 2NT — let them guess. The hand above is an example. If West has a minimum, East doesn't expect to make nine tricks. And yet, he should take the plunge and bid 3NT — or pass. With all those middle cards he is worth more than 11 points. Conversely, with all those pygmies, West isn't worth 14.

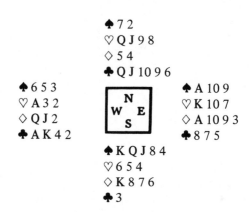

1

```
            ♠ 7 2
            ♡ Q J 9 8
            ◊ 5 4
            ♣ Q J 10 9 6
♠ 6 5 3              ♠ A 10 9
♡ A 3 2      N       ♡ K 10 7
◊ Q J 2    W   E     ◊ A 10 9 3
♣ A K 4 2    S       ♣ 8 7 5
            ♠ K Q J 8 4
            ♡ 6 5 4
            ◊ K 8 7 6
            ♣ 3
```

North leads the ♣Q, which holds, then the ♣J. West wins and takes the fateful diamond finesse, losing to South, who continues with his three top spades.

What hope is there of a ninth trick? The ♡QJ could be bare, so West cashes the ♡AK. No good. Resignedly he takes his winners, leaving himself with ♣A4 and dummy with ♡10 ♣8. The lead is in dummy. What of North? If he has kept the ♡Q he can only have one club, so the ♣A4 will score two tricks. Conversely, the ♡10 will be a winner.

Any beginner, without malice aforethought, might have squeezed North because the process was automatic. But observe the difference if, after the ♠K, South had switched. Go through the motions again. This time it's a 3-card ending and North has a card to spare, an *idle* card, not guarding anything. Now, however, West is no beginner and before cashing his winners he himself plays a second spade, ducking in dummy. The situation is as before. North's idle card having been removed, he is squeezed.

This is a vital part of all squeeze play. The mechanism only takes effect when all idle cards have gone, when declarer has conceded his inevitable losers — not before. If defenders haven't taken enough tricks, give them one! This is known in bridge parlance as *rectifying the count*.

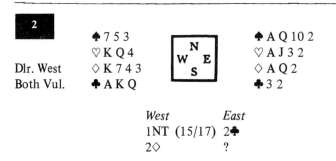

West	East
1NT (15/17)	2♣
2◇	?

Having found out, via Stayman, that there is no 4-4 major suit fit, East is just short of a direct raise to 6NT. Opposite a minimum no-trump (15) a combined total of 32 isn't quite enough with this shape. Admittedly, the three aces are worth more than 12 points, but against that the lack of intermediaries — only one ten and six midgets — is a flaw. This is always a factor to be taken into account in no-trumps.

All in all, East wants to invite a slam without committing himself, so he bids 4NT, leaving West to decide. Can this be interpreted as a Blackwood enquiry for aces? Alas, this does happen, but there is no excuse for it. Unless a suit has been agreed, if only by inference, as after a force or jump shift, 4NT is *always* quantitative, *never* Blackwood.

In sequences like:

1♠ – 3NT		1♠ – 1♡
	or	
4NT		2NT – 4NT

when the preceding bid is in no-trumps and no suit has been agreed, 4NT is an invitation — no more. With nothing to spare, partner passes. With a maximum no-trump, as above, the invitation is accepted with alacrity. Though the slam could still be played in a suit, the contract, after a quantitative 4NT, is usually 6NT.

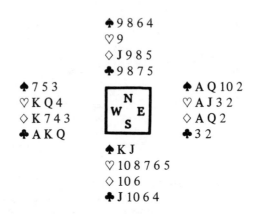

♠9 8 6 4
♥9
♦J 9 8 5
♣9 8 7 5

♠7 5 3
♥K Q 4
♦K 7 4 3
♣A K Q

♠A Q 10 2
♥A J 3 2
♦A Q 2
♣3 2

♠K J
♥10 8 7 6 5
♦10 6
♣J 10 6 4

Contract 6NT. North leads a club. If either the ♠J or ♠K is with North or if diamonds break 3-3, all will be well. A very promising situation, but the timing will be all-important.

West's first move is to finesse the ♠10. South wins with the ♠J and returns another club.

Before testing the diamonds declarer cashes his hearts, throwing a spade from hand. North, showing out the second time, parts with a club and two spades. Now come the diamonds. On the third round (♦K) South discards a heart.

It looks as if all will now hinge on finding North with the ♠K, but it would be poor technique to take the finesse before cashing the third top club. This brings about a 2-card ending in which declarer's ♠7 ♦7 face ♠AQ in dummy. Now, at last, he leads the ♠7, North following with the ♠9. Since his other card is known to be a diamond, the ♠Q can't win. So West goes up with the ♠A – and drops South's ♠K!

Had you counted the cards as they fell you would have known that South had one spade only left, perforce the king. This time counting wasn't vital. Next time it may be. So make a practice of it, for no habit is more rewarding.

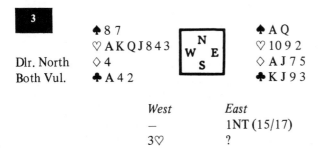

3

Dlr. North
Both Vul.

♠ 8 7
♡ A K Q J 8 4 3
◇ 4
♣ A 4 2

♠ A Q
♡ 10 9 2
◇ A J 7 5
♣ K J 9 3

West	East
—	1NT (15/17)
3♡	?

So far as East is concerned West may have no ambitions beyond game and is merely suggesting a suit contract in preference to no-trumps. With a doubleton in hearts he rebids 3NT. With more he agrees hearts. Should he then bid 4♡? He could do, but it costs nothing to cue-bid the ♠A. Obviously East hasn't suddenly discovered a new suit, so 3♠ agrees hearts by inference. Were West only looking for game he would now call 4♡, closing the bidding. Envisaging a slam, he bids 4♣ and East, in turn, shows his ◇A. He has a minimum no-trump but his cue-bids, pinpointing controls, promise no more. He could have a maximum 17, of course, and were this to consist of two aces and three kings, a grand slam would be cold. West is good enough to investigate and applies Blackwood. A suit, hearts, having been agreed, the 4NT is no longer quantitative as it would have been had West bid it directly over 1NT. Finding only one king opposite, West settles for 6♡.

West	East
—	1NT
3♡	3♠
4♣	4◇
4NT	5♡
5NT	6◇
6♡	

3

"Sorry, partner," said a contrite West, having gone down in a contract he should have made. It will be instructive to retrace his movements to find out where he went wrong, and above all, why.

North led the ◇K and the ◇A took the first trick, the ♡A the next one. A heart to dummy's ten drew the outstanding trump and now West ruffed a diamond. Back in dummy with the ♡9 he ruffed another. The ♣A and ♣2 to dummy's ♣J followed, losing to South's ♣Q. Had South returned a club or a spade declarer would have had his twelfth trick. Unfortunately, he had another diamond, and with the clubs 4-2 and the ♠K offside, the slam failed.

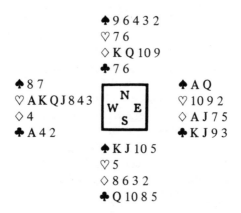

```
                    ♠ 9 6 4 3 2
                    ♡ 7 6
                    ◇ K Q 10 9
                    ♣ 7 6
     ♠ 8 7                              ♠ A Q
     ♡ A K Q J 8 4 3      N            ♡ 10 9 2
     ◇ 4            W         E        ◇ A J 7 5
     ♣ A 4 2             S            ♣ K J 9 3
                    ♠ K J 10 5
                    ♡ 5
                    ◇ 8 6 3 2
                    ♣ Q 10 8 5
```

What happened? The answer is that South shouldn't have had a diamond for a safe exit. West lost the vital tempo at trick two. The ♡A could have waited for a couple of seconds while he ruffed a diamond. With two trump entries he could have ruffed two more, leaving none for South — unless he had five, in which case North's ◇Q would have dropped.

West didn't lack technique so much as forethought. The time to make a plan is when dummy goes down, not later. Thinking, and counting ahead, should start before playing to the first trick.

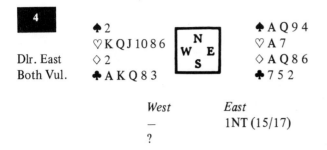

4

Dlr. East
Both Vul.

♠ 2
♡ K Q J 10 8 6
◇ 2
♣ A K Q 8 3

♠ A Q 9 4
♡ A 7
◇ A Q 8 6
♣ 7 5 2

West	East
–	1NT (15/17)
?	

This hand is made for the Gerber convention. A bid of 4♣ over 1NT or 2NT poses the question: how many aces? In response, 4◇ denies an ace, 4♡ shows one, 4♠ two, 4NT three and 5♣ all four.

West doesn't want to know whether East is minimum or maximum for his opening. He is interested solely in aces and that is the time, the *only* time, to use an ace-locating convention, be it Gerber over no-trump openings, or Blackwood on other occasions. West calls 4♣, hears 4NT – three aces – and confidently bids 7♡. Were the response 4♠ – two aces – he would stop in 6♡, and if East showed one ace only – 4♡ – West would simply pass.

In 7♡ he is prepared to find dummy with a doubleton club, for he could afford to ruff a club with the ♡A.

Occasions for Gerber do not come up very often, which means that it isn't abused so much as Blackwood. One of the convention's advantages is that it avoids all possible confusion between an enquiry for aces and a quantitative raise in no-trumps. Gerber can be used instead of Blackwood, but it is usual to confine it to no-trump openings and stick to Blackwood at other times.

4

North leads the ♠8 against 7♡. West goes up with dummy's ♠A, draws trumps and continues with the ♣A and ♣K. The second time North throws the ♠3 and thirteen tricks shrink to eleven. The diamond finesse would yield a twelfth, but where's the thirteenth?

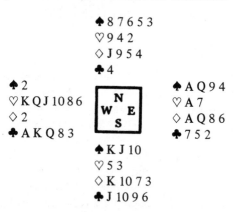

```
              ♠ 8 7 6 5 3
              ♡ 9 4 2
              ◇ J 9 5 4
              ♣ 4
♠ 2                              ♠ A Q 9 4
♡ K Q J 10 8 6      N           ♡ A 7
◇ 2            W       E        ◇ A Q 8 6
♣ A K Q 8 3        S           ♣ 7 5 2
              ♠ K J 10
              ♡ 5 3
              ◇ K 10 7 3
              ♣ J 10 9 6
```

No hope? Yes, if the ◇K is *wrong*, South, who appears to have the ♠K on the lead, will be the victim of a *progressive squeeze* in the 5-card ending.

(Immaterial)

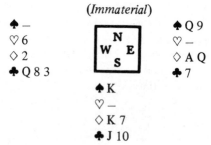

```
♠ —                              ♠ Q 9
♡ 6                N            ♡ —
◇ 2           W       E         ◇ A Q
♣ Q 8 3            S            ♣ 7
              ♠ K
              ♡ —
              ◇ K 7
              ♣ J 10
```

On the last heart dummy sheds the ♠9 and South the ◇7. The ◇A drops the ◇K and the ◇Q squeezes South in the black suits. Admittedly, misguessing, declarer can take the diamond finesse. If South parts with the ♠K, instead of the ◇7, the repeat squeeze is just as effective and West is spared all guesswork.

5			

Dlr. West
Both Vul.
E/W 30
Rubber Bridge

♠ 8 3
♡ A J 10 9 8
◇ A Q 6 3
♣ K 8

```
    N
 W     E
    S
```

♠ A J 9
♡ K Q 6
◇ K 9 4
♣ A 6 5 2

West	*East*
1♡	?

East bids 2♣. Over a 2♡ rebid he would call 4♡, one more than is needed for game. The inference is unmistakable. The jump to 4♡ cannot be designed to shut out opponents, for the 2♣ response gave them every chance to come in cheaply.

Suppose, however, that there were no part-score. The sequence − 2♣ followed by 4♡ − would be the same if East had an ace fewer. How can West tell the difference?

This brings to the fore a radical difference between two schools of thought. The moderns would first bid 2♣, then contrive an artificial reverse of 2♠ before raising hearts. The ancients would respond 3♣ the first time and, having shown a powerful hand, leave the rest to partner.

An interesting thought is that before the ancients, our primaeval ancestors followed the practice of the moderns! A force, a jump shift, proclaimed outstanding trump support or a solid suit, just as it does with the *avant garde* today. In fifty years, the wheel has turned full circle. Albert Morehead, one of America's greatest authorities, gave this as an example of a proper forcing response to 1♠:

♠A83 ♡AK754 ◇762 ♣A5.

Over a 2♡ response an aceless partner wouldn't readily envisage a slam, which could be cold. Alternatively, after 2♡, trying to catch up, West might soar too high.

Whether you force on hands too strong for a direct game, or insist on the rigid requirements of the moderns − and of Neanderthal Man − is a matter of style. Neither is necessarily right or wrong, but it is *always* wrong to play it one way if partner plays it the other.

5

$\spadesuit$ K 7 6 2
$\heartsuit$ 5 3 2
$\diamondsuit$ 5 2
$\clubsuit$ Q J 10 3

$\spadesuit$ 8 3
$\heartsuit$ A J 10 9 8
$\diamondsuit$ A Q 6 3
$\clubsuit$ K 8

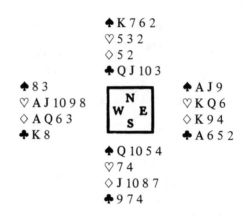

$\spadesuit$ A J 9
$\heartsuit$ K Q 6
$\diamondsuit$ K 9 4
$\clubsuit$ A 6 5 2

$\spadesuit$ Q 10 5 4
$\heartsuit$ 7 4
$\diamondsuit$ J 10 8 7
$\clubsuit$ 9 7 4

Against 6$\heartsuit$ North leads the $\clubsuit$Q, won in hand.

Declarer has eleven top tricks. A 3-3 diamond break would yield the twelfth. In addition, if the top honours in spades are divided and North has the $\spadesuit$10, finessing the $\spadesuit$9 could bring two tricks in spades. West draws trumps, and to combine both chances, the diamonds and the spades, begins with the latter, inserting the $\spadesuit$9. Unlucky. South wins with the $\spadesuit$10 and returns the $\diamondsuit$J. West takes two more rounds of diamonds and sees a spade from North on the third round. So that chance, too, has gone. Is all lost?

By no means. When everything else fails and declarer is short of a trick, he thinks of a squeeze. The first move is to cash the $\clubsuit$A and ruff a club. Now only one defender, North in this case, can guard clubs. West plays his last trump. After two clubs, a spade, three diamonds and five trumps, including the club ruff, North is down to two cards. Since he must keep a club his $\spadesuit$K is bare. West throws dummy's club, which has served its purpose, and the spotlight is on South. He can't part with a diamond since West still has one, so he too must bare his spade honour and dummy's $\spadesuit$AJ score the last two tricks.

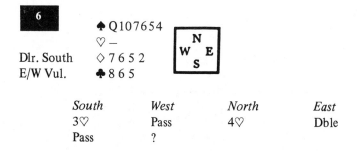

6

Dlr. South
E/W Vul.

♠ Q107654
♡ —
◇ 7 6 5 2
♣ 8 6 5

South	West	North	East
3♡	Pass	4♡	Dble
Pass	?		

By the nature of things, pre-emptive openings of three and four are overbids, advance sacrifices on hands without defence. This invites risks but puts opponents under pressure, depriving them of space to exchange information. The one must be measured against the other, the risk against the likely gain.

Various methods have been devised to counter pre-empts. Once popular, now out of fashion, is the Fishbein convention. To call for a take-out by partner the player in direct position, but not in the fourth, bids the cheapest suit, spades over hearts, hearts over diamonds.

Among the upper crust the *Optional Double* has all but ousted other methods. A double of a three bid or of four in a minor is *primarily* for take-out. Partner may, however, pass and should do so with a few high cards and no major to bid — or with a suitable holding in the enemy suit. An optional double should always be prepared for a major suit response, even on four pygmies. But there are no codes, no tables. Reason must always prevail over rules.

A double of 4♠ is for penalties. A double of 4♡ is *primarily* for penalties, but should show some tolerance for spades. Rarely, if ever, is a double based on trumps alone. The promise of other values is implicit and on a hand such as the above West should have no hesitation in bidding 4♠.

6

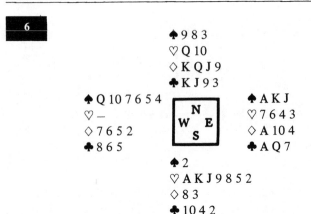

```
                    ♠ 9 8 3
                    ♡ Q 10
                    ◇ K Q J 9
                    ♣ K J 9 3
♠ Q 10 7 6 5 4                        ♠ A K J
♡ —                  N                ♡ 7 6 4 3
◇ 7 6 5 2        W       E            ◇ A 10 4
♣ 8 6 5              S                ♣ A Q 7
                    ♠ 2
                    ♡ A K J 9 8 5 2
                    ◇ 8 3
                    ♣ 10 4 2
```

Contract 4♠. North leads the ♣3. If the club finesse succeeds, West can see nine tricks — six spades, the ◇A and the ♣AQ. A 3-3 diamond break is against the odds and before he could ruff, dummy's trumps would surely be removed. Where, then, can declarer find his tenth trick?

The answer is a *Dummy Reversal*. West wins the first trick in dummy and ruffs a heart, crosses in trumps and ruffs another. Now comes the fateful club finesse, and when it wins, declarer ruffs a third heart, goes back to dummy with the ♣A and ruffs dummy's last heart with his last trump. All that remains is to go over to the ◇A and draw the last enemy trump. West has scored ten tricks with: four ruffs in the closed hand, dummy's three trumps, the ♣AQ and the ◇A.

The technique of the dummy reversal consists in ruffing in the hand long in trumps and drawing trump(s) from the hand opposite, usually dummy. Two requirements are essential: adequate entries and the master trump(s), in dummy at the end, to draw the enemy's. There are variations on the theme and situations in which the technique of the dummy-reversal can be combined with others.

7 ♥			
	♠ A 10 7 5 3 2		♠ K 9 8 6 4
	♡ Q	N	♡ A 8 4 2
Dlr. West	♢ A J 6	W E	♢ K 7
Both Vul.	♣ A Q 10	S	♣ J 5

West	North	East	South
1♠	Pass	4♠	Pass
5♣	Dble	5♡	Pass
5NT	Pass	?	

A direct bid of 5NT, *not preceded* by a Blackwood 4NT, is known as the *Grand Slam Force*, calling on partner to bid seven of the agreed suit if he has two of the three top honours. Without them he signs off in six. There are, however, refinements. This is a case in point.

North's double of 5♣ should have warned West not to be over-ambitious. An optimist by nature — or in urgent need of points in a match, perhaps — he visualises a grand slam, so long, of course, as the trumps are solid. With 5NT he puts the question.

Turn to East. Any response other than 7♠ denies two of the three top honours. But must it be 6♠? Yes, if his spades were Q986, but here, if West has five spades to the ace, the queen is likely to drop. To convey this message East responds not 6♠, but 6♡. This shows one of the three tops and a 5-card suit. With a 4-card suit and one top the bid would be 6♢. Were hearts the agreed suit, the corresponding responses would be 6♢ and 6♠. In diamonds 6♠ would show one top and five diamonds.

That is the original version of the G.S.F., as designed by Ely Culbertson more than fifty years ago. It has stood the test of time well. There are variations, but these needn't concern us. This convention, now in universal use, is sometimes called 'Josephine' after Mrs Culbertson, who is supposed to have invented it. In fact, like most experts, she opposed it when Ely introduced it.

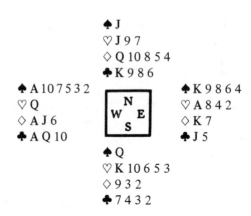

```
                    ♠ J
                    ♡ J 9 7
                    ◊ Q 10 8 5 4
                    ♣ K 9 8 6
♠ A 10 7 5 3 2                      ♠ K 9 8 6 4
♡ Q                N                ♡ A 8 4 2
◊ A J 6          W   E              ◊ K 7
♣ A Q 10           S               ♣ J 5
                    ♠ Q
                    ♡ K 10 6 5 3
                    ◊ 9 3 2
                    ♣ 7 4 3 2
```

North leads the ♣J against 7♠. Seeing dummy, West regrets his impetuous grand slam force, but it's too late. Where can he find thirteen tricks?

Declarer's thoughts turn to a *dummy reversal*. He has six trump tricks, but by ruffing three hearts in the closed hand the total may be raised to eight — dummy's five plus three ruffs. That's not quite enough, but it's a good start.

So, winning trick one with the ♠A, he cashes the ♡A, ruffs a heart and, crossing twice in trumps, ruffs two more.

The club finesse, after North's double isn't likely to succeed. Should he, then, pin his hopes on a finesse in diamonds? That's one way, but there may be a better one, especially if, as here, North shows out on the fourth heart. Presumably longer in diamonds than South, he is more likely to have the ◊Q. West takes that view, and after ruffing dummy's last heart with his last trump, he cashes the ♣A — the key move. Next he crosses to the ◊K and plays off dummy's two remaining trumps, discarding his ♣Q10. Two cards are left. Dummy's ◊7 ♣J face declarer's ◊AJ. And North? Unless he has thrown his ♣K his ◊Q must drop.

North's fatuous double of 5♣ was an expensive noise. Such doubles often help declarer, rarely partner.

8

Dlr. West
Both Vul.

♠ J 4 2
♡ A K Q 1096
◇ A 5
♣ K J

```
    N
 W     E
    S
```

♠ A Q 10
♡ 7 4
◇ 9 8
♣ A Q 10 9 7 6

West	East
1♡	2♣
4♡	?

The partnership must be in the slam zone and the unsophisticated East may think of Blackwood. An unworthy thought, for how would it help him to know that partner had two aces? West's hand could be: ♠94 ♡AKQ1096 ◇AKQ ♣54, same strength as before. A grand slam would then be an absurd proposition and even a small slam would be no certainty. Yet with West's existing hand 7♡ is an admirable contract.

Blackwood 4NT should only be invoked when the number of aces, and nothing else, is the prime consideration (see 2 and 3). It should never be used as an invitation to a slam. There are better ways of doing that.

Here, over 4♡, East makes a cue-bid of 4♠. West's natural response is 5◇, but the ◇A won't run away and 5♣ is more constructive. Having the ♣A himself, East has an idea of what's happening, but with two diamond losers he can do no more than sign off in 5♡. This is where West's 5♣ brings its reward, allowing him to bid 5NT, the grand slam force, calling on East to bid 7♣ with two of the three top honours. The sequence will be:

West	East
1♡	2♣
4♡	4♠
5♣	5♡
5NT	7♣
7♡	

8

North leads the ◇K. West wins and lays down the ♡AK. The second time North shows out. At first sight there's no way of avoiding a trump loser, but there is a mechanism, simple once you've mastered it, which allows you to do it.

West reduces his trumps to South's level, eliminates the side suits and leads from dummy, forcing South, with only trumps left, to ruff in front of him.

Here West needs three entries, so the spade finesse must be right. Defenders' hands could be:

> North: ♠ K53   ♡2   ◇KQ10763   ♣542
> South: ♠9876   ♡J853   ◇J42   ♣83

Let's go through the motions. After the ♡K West cashes two clubs, ruffs a club — first trump reduction — and, finessing the ♠10, ruffs a second club. Trumps are now equal. Back in dummy with a second finesse in spades, West has two more clubs to lead. This is the 3-card ending:

(Immaterial)

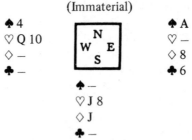

If South throws his ◇J West discards the ♠4 and the ♠A is the killer.

Had South ruffed the penultimate club — on which West threw his diamond loser — West would have over-ruffed, drawn South's last trump and gone over to the ♠A to cash the last club.

9	♠ A J 9 8 6 5		♠ K 7 4 3
	♡ 2	N	♡ A 10
Dlr. North	◇ K 6 4 2	W E	◇ A 5 3
E/W Vul.	♣ 8 3	S	♣ A K Q 6

West	North	East	South
—	Pass	2NT	3♡
3♠	4♡	5♣	Pass
6♠	7♡	*Pass*	Pass
?			

In points East has a minimum 2NT, but with so many controls and every high card working he is worth more, especially when a slam is in prospect. Always undervalued at 4 points, an ace is worth appreciably more in the slam zone than a KJ or two queens.

East's 5♣ is a cue-bid showing spade support, as well as the ♣A, and is therefore encouraging. West promptly accepts the invitation. He has no wasted values.

At the vulnerability it's hardly surprising that, having found a fit, North-South should sacrifice at the seven level. Uncertain what course to take, East makes a *forcing pass*, leaving the decision to partner. Without an ace West would double.

Even if there's a finesse to take the grand slam may be a better proposition than an inadequate penalty. There is no doubt, of course, that East has three aces. Otherwise he would have doubled as a warning to West.

The *forcing pass*, therefore, invites the grand slam. West accepts.

9

North leads the ♡9. Declarer's first concern is a 3-0 trump break. Should either defender have ♠Q102, the queen can only be caught if the void is with North. West starts with the ♠K.

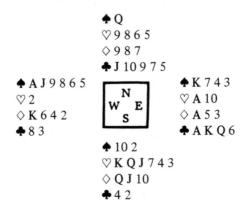

```
                    ♠ Q
                    ♡ 9 8 6 5
                    ◇ 9 8 7
                    ♣ J 10 9 7 5
   ♠ A J 9 8 6 5          ┌─────────┐      ♠ K 7 4 3
   ♡ 2                    │    N    │      ♡ A 10
   ◇ K 6 4 2              │  W   E  │      ◇ A 5 3
   ♣ 8 3                  │    S    │      ♣ A K Q 6
                          └─────────┘
                    ♠ 10 2
                    ♡ K Q J 7 4 3
                    ◇ Q J 10
                    ♣ 4 2
```

Trumps are no problem, but West can only see twelve tricks. How can he conjure up a thirteenth?

Having drawn trumps in two rounds, he cashes the ♣AKQ, and as soon as South shows out, West could put his hand down and claim. Visualise the ending. After a heart, three clubs and five spades, North is down to four cards, the ◇987 ♣J, and there's a sixth spade to come. What does he discard? He has to keep the ♣J, for the ♣6 is still in dummy. So he sheds a diamond. West throws dummy's ♣6, which has served its purpose, and turns the heat on South. He must keep the ♡K, for the ♡10 remains in dummy flanked by ◇A5, so he too comes down to two diamonds, and West's last three cards, ◇K64, are all winners.

North-South have no defence against a *double squeeze*.

10

♠ A K 7 5		♠ J 10 6
♡ A K 6 2	N	♡ 7 4
◇ K	W E	◇ A J 10 9 8 7
♣ A 9 8 2	S	♣ 10 4

Dlr. West
Love All

Beware of the 4-4-4-1 pattern. It doesn't come up more than three times in a hundred deals, but when it does it poses problems, and the bigger the hand, the tougher the problem.

The West hand above is made for the Roman Two-Diamonds Convention. On the second round West bids his singleton or void, so a 4-4 fit in any other suit quickly comes to light. Here, however, you are not playing the Roman, so what should you bid?

You have the strength for 2NT, but not the shape. And yet it may be the best way to ensure that a 4-4 fit in a major isn't lost. The *correct* opening is undoubtedly 1♣, followed by a jump rebid in a major. Yes, but which one? If over, say, 1◇ you bid 2♡, no bid in spades thereafter would show a genuine suit and a 4-4 spade fit could be lost. Should your jump rebid be in spades you could lose a heart fit.

If, an anarchist by nature, you open 2NT — as I would be sorely tempted to do — take care to cover your tracks. Should you go down as dummy, append the ♡2 discreetly to the ◇K. Anyone can make that sort of mistake, but to open 2NT with a singleton is distinctly non-U.

The final contract here will be 3NT anyway, and it would be the same if you played the Roman Two-Diamonds — which, incidentally, can be incorporated into any system.

10

North leads the ♠3. How should West play to make certain of his contract regardless of the distribution?

The automatic reflex is to put up dummy's ♠J, making certain of three spade tricks. If you look ahead, however, you will see that this could be, probably would be, fatal, for the ♠J10 provides the only entry to dummy's diamonds. If South has the ♠Q, he will play low. If the queen is with North you are no better off.

So play *low* from dummy at trick one, win with the ♠A(K), over-take the ◇K and lead another, clearing the suit. Whatever the return you will lead a low spade, losing to the ♠Q, but you will have a certain entry to four good diamonds. Your losers will be the ◇Q, the ♠Q and two clubs.

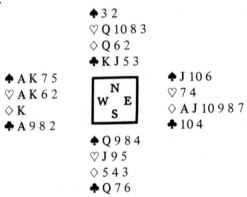

```
              ♠ 3 2
              ♡ Q 10 8 3
              ◇ Q 6 2
              ♣ K J 5 3
♠ A K 7 5                      ♠ J 10 6
♡ A K 6 2        N            ♡ 7 4
◇ K           W     E         ◇ A J 10 9 8 7
♣ A 9 8 2        S            ♣ 10 4
              ♠ Q 9 8 4
              ♡ J 9 5
              ◇ 5 4 3
              ♣ Q 7 6
```

It's an easy hand but reinforces a lesson many players tend to forget — at the table. No matter how quickly you may play later, take your time at trick one. That's when you should think the hand out. And if you are dummy, don't flick a singleton automatically on the opening lead. If declarer stops to think, as he should do, he may give the impression of having a problem when he has none, or betray a weakness where he has one.

11

Dlr. East
N/S Vul.

♠ A 8 6 5
♡ 6 5
◇ A 7 4
♣ K 10 5 2

	N	
W		E
	S	

♠ K 7 2
♡ K Q 8 3
◇ 8
♣ A Q J 7 3

West	East
–	1♣
1♠	2♣
3♣	3♡
3NT	?

Having fully described his hand, the orthodox East will now pass. The heretic may well prefer the awkward 4-3 spade fit to no-trumps. In a suit contract the singleton diamond offers ruffing value and is a source of strength. In no-trumps it's a grave liability. Opponents are marked with length in the suit, so a favourable, or even a neutral lead is unlikely. And unless declarer can reel off nine tricks quickly, defenders may come to five first.

There is, however, an alternative to both spades and no-trumps – clubs. East can almost bid 5♣ himself, but if in doubt he can consult West with – 4♣. West would have bid the same way with: ♠AQJ8 ♡65 ◇A74 ♣10542. Now he would bid 4♠. With the cards as above he would prefer 5♣.

Exchange the ♡3 for the ◇3 and 3NT becomes the better contract. The diamond lead is less certain and if the suit breaks 4-4 (32 per cent) declarer will have time to set up his ninth trick in hearts. In the event of the more likely 5-3 division (47 per cent) the player with the ♡A may not have the long diamonds.

The moral is: beware of singletons in no-trumps – and don't always look askance at minors.

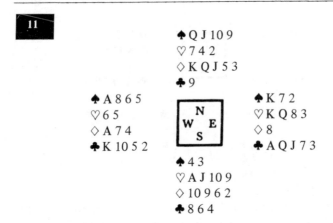

11

♠ Q J 10 9
♡ 7 4 2
◇ K Q J 5 3
♣ 9

♠ A 8 6 5   ♠ K 7 2
♡ 6 5   ♡ K Q 8 3
◇ A 7 4   ◇ 8
♣ K 10 5 2   ♣ A Q J 7 3

N
W E
S

♠ 4 3
♡ A J 10 9
◇ 10 9 6 2
♣ 8 6 4

Observe that 3NT can't be made. The ◇A will be quickly driven out and before declarer can set up a heart for his ninth trick, defenders will have four diamonds to cash. Conversely, neither 4♠ nor 5♣ should present any problems.

In 4♠ declarer wins the trump lead in dummy, cashes the ◇A, ruffs a diamond and getting back with the ♣10, ruffs another. Next he leads a club, intending to lay down the ♠A before going on with the clubs. North can ruff, of course, and force West with a diamond. It won't hurt him for he will cash the ♠A and lead another club, keeping a move ahead all the time. It would be distinctly unlucky to find the same defender with a singleton club and a doubleton spade.

In 5♣ only carelessness could rob East of the contract. To come to eleven tricks he needs two heart ruffs in dummy, so he cannot afford more than one round of trumps before broaching the hearts. A third trump from South, when he is in with the ♡A, would kill the contract.

Even if West had the ◇K, instead of the ♣K, 3NT would depend on the club finesse, while 5♣ would still be pretty cold. Now, however, declarer couldn't afford even one round of trumps before driving out the ♡A.

The simpler the convention, the more it lends itself to abuse. Stayman, second only to Blackwood in popularity, is no exception.

Once upon a time opening 1NT risked losing a 4-4 fit in a major. To overcome this handicap an artificial bid of 2♣ by responder allows opener to show a 4-card major. Without one he bids 2◇. Paternity for this convention is claimed on both sides of the Atlantic, but it is generally recognised as the brain-child of Sam Stayman of New York.

On many hands Stayman is invaluable, bringing to light a major suit fit when a no-trump contract couldn't succeed. But useful though it be, it isn't compulsory. You do not have to invoke Stayman just because you have a 4-card major. This would be a case in point.

```
    ♠ J 4 2              ♠ Q 8 6
    ♡ A Q 7 2     N      ♡ K 8 6 3
    ◇ K 10 3    W   E    ◇ Q J 5
    ♣ A Q 3       S      ♣ K 10 4
```

          West   *East*
          1NT (15/17)   ?

The opener may have four hearts, as above, but he has advertised a balanced hand and, unless he has a doubleton, there will be no more tricks in hearts than in no-trumps — and one more to get. With an honour in every suit, and no weak spots anywhere, East should bid 3NT. With a worthless doubleton, it would be different. As you can see, only bad breaks can defeat 3NT. In hearts declarer has the same nine tricks and no more.

Stayman isn't forcing for more than one round. In some schools — not in mine — a bid of 2♡ or 2♠ by responder over opener's 2◇ shows more strength than an ordinary weakness take-out. That's a matter of style. As with all conventions there's a price to pay for Stayman. It conveys information to defenders, as well as to partner, and they may become the chief beneficiaries.

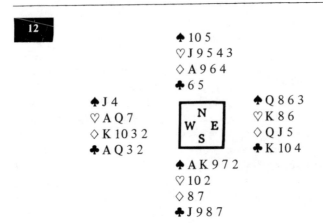

12

♠ 10 5
♡ J 9 5 4 3
◇ A 9 6 4
♣ 6 5

♠ J 4
♡ A Q 7
◇ K 10 3 2
♣ A Q 3 2

♠ Q 8 6 3
♡ K 8 6
◇ Q J 5
♣ K 10 4

♠ A K 9 7 2
♡ 10 2
◇ 8 7
♣ J 9 8 7

Two twos have changed places in West's hand. The ♠2 has moved down to the diamonds and the ♡2 has joined the clubs. East's ♡3 is now a spade. Otherwise they are the same hands as on the previous page and again West opens 1NT.

If East makes the recommended bid of 3NT, North will doubtless lead a heart and, after driving out the ◇A, West will quickly wrap up nine tricks.

Now suppose that East applies Stayman and, finding no fit, then bids 3NT. What will North lead now? A heart looks dangerous for there may be four in dummy. Begging to be led is the ♠10. West can't have more than three spades and may have a doubleton; dummy has four at most and may have fewer. So South must have at least four spades and, sitting over dummy, his cards should be well-placed.

The devastating spade lead — which North wouldn't have found, but for Stayman — is the one and only to kill the contract. West wins the first trick with the ♠J, but North comes in with the ◇A and a second spade yields the defence four more tricks.

Duck the ♠10? Then what if South has the ◇A?

13

Not allowed as a rule in rubber bridge, but widely used in competitions is the *transfer bid* over no-trump openings. With a 5- or 6-card suit responder calls the one *below* it — 2◇ if the suit is hearts, 2♡ if it's spades. Stayman remains unaffected and 2♠ is transferred to 3♣. Devised originally by Oswald Jacoby more than thirty years ago, the prime purpose of transfers is to steer the opening lead towards the stronger hand. Playing the weak no-trump this advantage is largely lost, especially at game level, for responder is likely to be as strong as opener, if not stronger. Transfers have, however, other attractions, allowing each partner, in turn, to show added values. This would be a case in point:

♠ A Q 4 2   ♠ K 10 8 6 5
♡ K 7 5   ♡ 8 4 2
◇ 10 5 2   ◇ A K 4 3
♣ A 8 3   ♣ 6

```
      N
   W     E
      S
```

Over West's 1NT (weak) East has plenty to spare for a 2♠ take-out, yet not enough to contract for game without taking a considerable gamble. He bids 2♡, a transfer. With a doubleton spade, West would still have to bid 2♠. Anything else will, therefore, show something better. Having a perfect fit, West bids 3♣. On a minimum East will sign off. Here he encourages with 3◇. West could still settle for 3♠, but he has enough to call the game.

Transpose the ◇K and ◇10 and you would have the same sequence over a strong no-trump.

I hasten to add that there are many variations and deviations. The treatment shown above is only one of several. Partnership understanding is, of course, of the essence, but the principle itself is valuable — so long as the practice is kept simple.

```
                          ♠ J 7
                          ♡ A Q 9 3
                          ◇ J 9 8 6
                          ♣ K Q 10
         ♠ A Q 4 2                          ♠ K 10 8 6 5
         ♡ K 7 5          ┌─────────┐       ♡ 8 4 2
         ◇ 10 5 2         │    N    │       ◇ A K 4 3
         ♣ A 8 3       W  │ W     E │  E    ♣ 6
                          │    S    │
                          └─────────┘
                          ♠ 9 3
                          ♡ J 10 6
                          ◇ Q 7
                          ♣ J 9 7 5 4 2
```

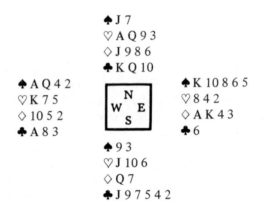

Contract 4♠. North leads the ♣K.

West wins, ruffs a club, draws trumps in two rounds and ruffs another club. Next he cashes the ◇AK and exits with a third diamond. So long as North wins the trick, declarer is home, regardless of the diamond break. If, as above, North has a fourth diamond to play, West will discard a heart and wait for North's next lead to give him his tenth trick, a heart to the king or a ruff and discard.

Should trumps split 3-1, South having three, West will probably have to find the ♡A on the right side. He can still try for a partial elimination, however, taking two rounds of trumps only before playing diamonds. This time, though, a 4-2 break would spoil the end-play. All in all, 4♠ is an excellent contract, easier to reach with transfers than without them. A possible Stayman sequence would be:

1NT	2♣
2♠	3♠
?	

With such good trumps, West should bid 4♠.

14

♠ A K 6
♡ A J 10 9 7
Dlr. East   ◊ A Q 10
Both Vul.   ♣ Q 10

```
        N
      W   E
        S
```

West	North	East	South
—	—	Pass	Pass
1♡	Pass	3♡	Pass
?			

Problems in textbooks, and in articles too for that matter, invariably presuppose the best defence. That, in turn, assumes that the contract can be made by the best declarer-play. In real life neither should be taken for granted. Errors by both sides are not infrequent and wrong views abound, even among the élite.

It is true that if a contract is reached after a scientific sequence, pinpointing every honour and every doubleton, defenders' room for error is severely restricted. But if the bidding gives nothing away, the defence is in the dark, and by the time the light breaks through it may be too late.

On West's hand above, it is difficult to keep out of 6♡. Don't try too hard. Yes, you may have two club losers — if a club is led. But how can you find out? Blackwood? But you don't need the ♣A — a single-ton or the ♣K will do. A series of cue-bids? That might do it, but there's much to be said for taking a calculated liberty and bidding 6♡ in one bound. Should partner turn up with two losing clubs, it would be a sad but not uncommon case of duplication and you can plead bad luck.

Opponents have a choice of three suits to lead, with trumps as favourites on the bidding, so the *real* odds can be no worse than 50-50 and are probably a good deal better.

There's nothing shameful in calling what may be, in theory, a bad slam, if in practice you have a good chance of making it.

14

```
              ♠ 7 4
              ♡ 5 2
              ◇ 6 4 3 2
              ♣ J 7 5 3 2
♠ A K 6                           ♠ Q 8 5 3
♡ A J 10 9 7    ┌─────────┐       ♡ K Q 8 6
◇ A Q 10        │   N     │       ◇ K J 8
♣ Q 10          │ W   E   │       ♣ 9 4
                │   S     │
                └─────────┘
              ♠ J 10 9 2
              ♡ 4 3
              ◇ 9 7 5
              ♣ A K 8 6
```

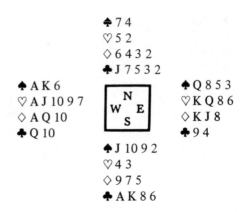

North leads a trump against 6♡.

At first sight, the slam appears to depend on a 3-3 spade break, only one chance in three. That, however, won't run away. With four spades on view in dummy, a careless discard is unlikely, but there may be other possibilities. Declarer plays out his red winners to the bitter end — five hearts and three diamonds. Coming down to five cards, South is under pressure. He must retain all four spades for he knows, or should know by now, West's holding. So he lets go one of his top clubs, hoping that North has the ♣Q.

That discard should tell West all he needs to know. Obviously South would have retained the ♣AK intact unless he had four spades. So West leads the ♣10, brings down the ♣A(K) and claims.

A bad contract? Certainly, but a good gamble, so don't be too hard on the result merchant when he defends his leap to 6♡. And don't forget in the auction to give yourself the best chance in the play.

15

Dlr. West
N/S Vul.

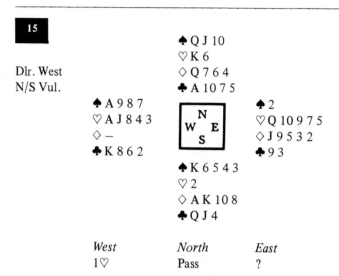

♠ Q J 10
♡ K 6
◇ Q 7 6 4
♣ A 10 7 5

♠ A 9 8 7
♡ A J 8 4 3
◇ —
♣ K 8 6 2

♠ 2
♡ Q 10 9 7 5
◇ J 9 5 3 2
♣ 9 3

♠ K 6 5 4 3
♡ 2
◇ A K 10 8
♣ Q J 4

West	North	East
1♡	Pass	?

The values for a direct raise to game depend on style and system, but few players would consider East good enough to stretch to 4♡. Yet this may well be the right time for the wrong bid. The singleton spade is the reason. Whoever has the spades starts with a bid advantage, being able to outbid opponents at the same level. East fears that over 2♡, even over 3♡, opponents would come in and if they did on the hand above, they would easily make 4♠. So he soars to 4♡. That's too high a barrage for the opposition.

North leads the ♠Q. West sees three possible losers, a heart and two clubs, but this presupposes ruffing five black cards in dummy and a trump from South at any stage would be embarrassing. So he lets the ♠Q hold, wins the spade continuation, discarding a club from dummy, ruffs a spade and leads a club. If South has the ♣A, four ruffs in dummy will suffice. If North has it, he cannot lead a trump profitably and West will be able to ruff all his losers.

Into the Fray

The initiation is over. We can now set about putting theory into practice, bearing in mind as we bid the hands on one page that we shall have to play them overleaf and make our contracts.

In standard textbooks the chapter headings, like the answers at the back of school books, give too much away. The reader knows what's expected of him — a slam, a squeeze, a safety play. Half his troubles are over. At the table he would get no advance information. With plenty of weapons in his armoury he would have to pick the right one each time. To vary the metaphor, his cupboard is well-stocked with potent medicines, but he must diagnose the complaint before applying the cure. And that is what he will be doing a hundred times in these pages. There will be no shortage of complaints, I promise.

Unless otherwise stated, the scoring is as at rubber bridge or in teams events. Simplicity is throughout the order of the day, for it isn't enough to master the skills of winning. The process must be painless. Hard work is, no doubt, highly commendable elsewhere — but not at the bridge table. Still less in a textbook. So remember Talleyrand's advice to ambitious young men in the diplomatic service: "Above all, not too much zeal." Or science, he might have added.

16		
	♠ K 7 5	♠ A Q J 10
	♡ A J 10	♡ 5 3 2
Dlr. West	◇ A K 7 3	◇ Q 8 4
Both Vul.	♣ A Q 10	♣ K 9 5

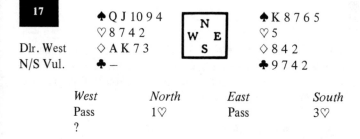

West	East
2NT	3♣
3◇	3♠
3NT	6NT

This is a Baron sequence. East's 3♣ looks for a 4-4 fit, not just in a major as with Stayman, but in *any* suit. West shows his 4-card suit and, with two suits, bids them upwards. East, in turn, bids his suit on the second round. No fit having been found, East settles for 6NT.

Had West's 4-card suit been clubs his response would have been 3NT.

17		
	♠ Q J 10 9 4	♠ K 8 7 6 5
	♡ 8 7 4 2	♡ 5
Dlr. West	◇ A K 7 3	◇ 8 4 2
N/S Vul.	♣ —	♣ 9 7 4 2

West	North	East	South
Pass	1♡	Pass	3♡
?			

Though West isn't quite good enough to open, paradoxically he should now come in with 3♠. The reason is that partner's hand has improved enormously. He cannot have more than one heart, so he should have at least three spades, maybe more. Having found a fit, opponents will probably bid 4♡ and 4♠ should prove a cheap sacrifice or even a make. Alternatively, North-South will be pushed into 5♡.

16

North leads the ♠9. West intends to finesse twice in hearts and will score twelve tricks unless North has both the missing honours. Alternatively, a 3-3 diamond break will suffice. But it's better still to combine both chances. First take a heart finesse, then test the diamonds. Unless they are 3-3, finesse again in hearts.

Simple, and yet West can fall into a trap, set unwittingly by himself. If he begins by playing off his spades, the fourth one will squeeze him in the red suits, which would be very undignified, to say the least.

17

Against 4♠ North leads the ♠A, the ♡K, then the ♣K. West has ten tricks: seven on a cross-ruff, a trump and the ◇AK. But he must be careful. On the fourth heart, ruffed in dummy, South discards a diamond, and the North-South hands may well be:

> North: ♠ A   ♡ AK963   ◇ J965   ♣ KQ10
> South: ♠ 32   ♡ QJ10   ◇ Q10   ♣ AJ8653

West ruffs dummy's last club with his last spade, but he cannot get back to dummy to draw the last trump. So his second diamond trick is ruffed.

The answer is to cash the ◇AK before embarking on a cross-ruff. It's a golden rule in all such situations: cash the winners in the side-suit(s) before you set about ruffing the losers.

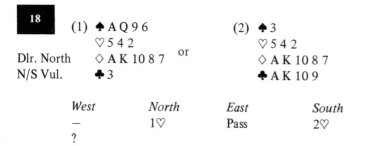

18

(1) ♠ A Q 9 6
    ♡ 5 4 2
Dlr. North   ◇ A K 10 8 7   or
N/S Vul.   ♣ 3

(2) ♠ 3
    ♡ 5 4 2
    ◇ A K 10 8 7
    ♣ A K 10 9

West	North	East	South
—	1♡	Pass	2♡
?			

In (1) West has the spades (see **14**) and that makes all the difference.
He doubles, knowing that East, who must be short in hearts, won't
therefore be short in spades, too, and that he will bid them even with
longer clubs. Though (2) is stronger, there can be no double without
spades. If West wants to come in, his only bid is 2NT, calling for a
minor and denying spades by implication.

19

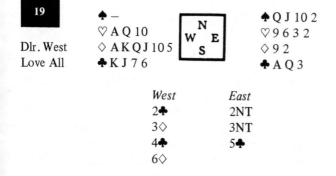

♠ —
♡ A Q 10
Dlr. West   ◇ A K Q J 10 5
Love All   ♣ K J 7 6

♠ Q J 10 2
♡ 9 6 3 2
◇ 9 2
♣ A Q 3

West	East
2♣	2NT
3◇	3NT
4♣	5♣
6◇	

The 2NT response is positive and usually promises 8-9 scattered points,
but with an ace and a king, 7 suffice.

West is wary because East could have wasted values in spades. Hence
the exploratory 4♣. After a raise to 5♣ there's no further problem — in
the bidding.

18

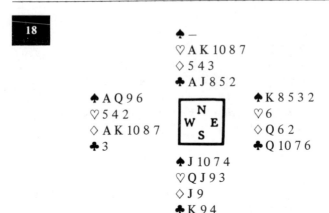

♠ —
♡ A K 10 8 7
♢ 5 4 3
♣ A J 8 5 2

♠ A Q 9 6
♡ 5 4 2
♢ A K 10 8 7
♣ 3

♠ K 8 5 3 2
♡ 6
♢ Q 6 2
♣ Q 10 7 6

♠ J 10 7 4
♡ Q J 9 3
♢ J 9
♣ K 9 4

East bids 4♠ over 4♡. South doubles and leads a heart to the ♡K, and the ♡A follows. The 4-0 trump break being the main danger, East starts with the ♠K, for only so can he pick up all the trumps.

North-South could have sacrificed cheaply, but with the spades against them, they couldn't win.

19

North leads the ♣10 and prospects are rosy. If South has either the ♡K or ♡J, all is well. That's 3-1 on declarer, and yet he can do a lot better. Winning the second round of trumps in dummy, he leads the ♠Q, throwing the ♡10, unless South covers. Let North win. Whatever he returns, West draws trumps, crosses in clubs, plays the ♠J and takes a ruffing finesse, placing South with the second top spade. Still only 3-1? Virtually 100 per cent. With ♠AK North would have led the suit instead of a club. His hand could be: ♠A7643 ♡KJ4 ♢83 ♣1098.

20 (a) ♠ A Q 6   (b) ♠ A Q 6   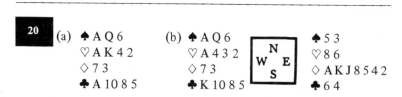   ♠ 5 3
      ♡ A K 4 2   ♡ A 4 3 2   ♡ 8 6
      ◊ 7 3   ◊ 7 3   ◊ A K J 8 5 4 2
      ♣ A 10 8 5   ♣ K 10 8 5   ♣ 6 4

West bids 1NT. What should East say if (a) it's strong (15/17)? (b) weak (12/14)?

The point count is a good servant, but a bad master. With 8 points East may have just enough for game opposite 17, but not nearly enough opposite 13. Both times, however, he should bid 3NT. If the diamonds work, and partner can't have a singleton, nine tricks will probably materialise, and it's *tricks*, not points, that count.

21

Dlr. West
Love All

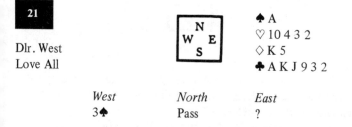

♠ A
♡ 10 4 3 2
◊ K 5
♣ A K J 9 3 2

West	*North*	*East*
3♣	Pass	?

Whether you should bid 4♣ or pass depends largely on West's style. On Mondays and Tuesdays, with a daring partner who pre-empts on seven to the queen-knave, pass and expect to go down. On Wednesdays, with a solid bidder, raise to 4♣. The bid you mustn't make with anyone, at any time, is 3NT. Since the pre-emptive bidder is unlikely to have an entry, partner's values in no-trumps may be zero.

20

The ♠2 is led. Winning, West plays the ◇7 and North the ◇9. And dummy? So long as South follows it won't matter, for the rest of the suit will be good. What if the ◇J is played, wins and South shows out? Now the diamonds will bring in three tricks only. The ◇9 should be ducked. If South shows out, the marked finesse will bring in six tricks.

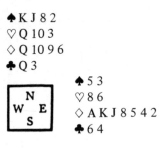

```
            ♠ K J 8 2
            ♡ Q 10 3
            ◇ Q 10 9 6
            ♣ Q 3
                        ♠ 5 3
         N              ♡ 8 6
      W     E           ◇ A K J 8 5 4 2
         S              ♣ 6 4
```

21

```
♠ K Q J 10 8 7          ♠ A
♡ Q J 9          N      ♡ 10 4 3 2
◇ J 10 4      W     E   ◇ K 5
♣ 4              S      ♣ A K J 9 3 2
```

There's a play for 4♠, but let's try to bring home a reprehensible 3NT. South leads the ◇6 to North's ace and the ◇3 comes back. With the spades blocked, is there much hope?

The contract is unbeatable — so long as East jettisoned his ◇K on the ace! It couldn't cost for there was only one hold-up in diamonds anyway. If defenders persist with diamonds, the ♠A is thrown on the ◇J, unblocking. If, after the ◇Q, they switch, there's time to set up a heart entry to the spades.

North has a counter — if he finds it! At trick one he plays *low*.

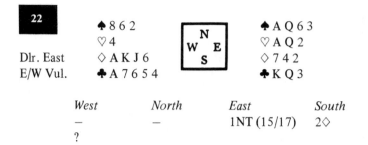

22

	♠ 8 6 2		♠ A Q 6 3
	♡ 4		♡ A Q 2
Dlr. East	◇ A K J 6		◇ 7 4 2
E/W Vul.	♣ A 7 6 5 4		♣ K Q 3

West	North	East	South
–	–	1NT (15/17)	2◇
?			

A splendid double? *Too* splendid! North-South must have at least eight hearts between them, maybe ten, so someone, probably North, will bid 2♡. If East doubles, West will feel unhappy and should he then bid 3NT he must expect an unfriendly lead. West should bid 3NT at once, without giving any information to the enemy.

23

	♠ A Q J		♠ 10 9 7
	♡ A K Q		♡ 9 8
Dlr. West	◇ 6 3		◇ A J 10 8 4
Both Vul.	♣ 9 8 5 4 2		♣ Q J 10

What should West open? Playing a weak no-trump (12/14), there's no problem. West bids 1♣, and over, say, 1◇, rebids 1NT, showing a balanced hand with 15-16 points, too much for an opening 1NT. Playing a strong no-trump (15/17) there's just too much for a 1NT rebid and not enough for 2NT. So West opens 1NT, not ideal with nothing in diamonds, but the best bid available.

East is worth a raise to 2NT, but with all those middle cards couldn't be blamed for bidding game. A point to bear in mind is that one is hardly ever doubled on that bidding.

22

Against 3NT South leads the ◊10, North discarding the ♡3. East tests the clubs. The second time South shows out. Declarer sees eight tricks: six in the minors and two aces. He needs a finesse, yet both kings may be wrong.

He makes certain of 3NT by cashing his minor-suit winners and exiting with a diamond. South can cash two more, but must then lead a spade or a heart.

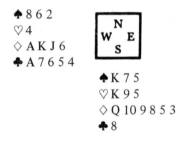

```
        ♠ 8 6 2
        ♡ 4
        ◊ A K J 6
        ♣ A 7 6 5 4
                        ♠ K 7 5
                        ♡ K 9 5
                        ◊ Q 10 9 8 5 3
                        ♣ 8
```

23

Against 3NT North leads the ♡5 to South's ♡J. At trick two, declarer plays a club on which North discards the ♠3. South wins and returns the ♡3. How should West proceed?

He can see eight tricks. The spade finesse would yield the ninth if the king is with South. If not, North might have two heart winners to cash. Declarer cannot afford to cross to the ◊A to take the finesse, so, at trick four, he plays the ♣Q from hand. Whoever has the ♠K will doubtless knock out his last heart stopper, but now he can set up the clubs in safety. Either South won't have a heart to return or the suit will have been broken harmlessly 4-4. A likely set-up would be:

North: ♠K5432 ♡107654 ◊752 ♣—
South: ♠86 ♡J32 ◊KQ9 ♣AK763

24

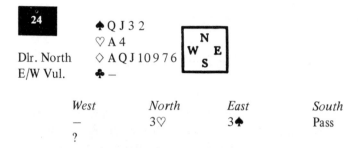

Dlr. North
E/W Vul.

♠ Q J 3 2
♡ A 4
◇ A Q J 10 9 7 6
♣ —

West	North	East	South
—	3♡	3♠	Pass
?			

You expect to make a grand slam or to go down in a small one. All will hinge on the diamond finesse, attractive odds, for you will gain 2210, at duplicate scoring, or lose a mere 850, the vulnerable game plus 200.

Go to it. Make sure first, though, that partner has the ♠AK, so bid 5NT, calling on him to bid the grand slam with two of the three top trump honours.

25

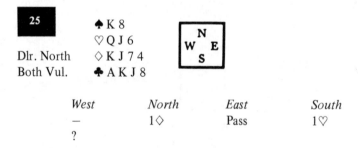

Dlr. North
Both Vul.

♠ K 8
♡ Q J 6
◇ K J 7 4
♣ A K J 8

West	North	East	South
—	1◇	Pass	1♡
?			

Are you tempted to bid 1NT? For once you must resist temptation. Once both opponents have bid, even though each, in turn, on minimum values, a 1NT overcall on a balanced hand serves little purpose. If you have 18 points, partner isn't likely to have more than 2 and may have none. Having to play away from your honours your values will shrink trick by trick. Pass.

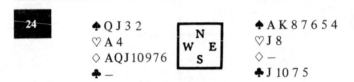

24

♠ Q J 3 2
♡ A 4
◊ A Q J 10 9 7 6
♣ —

♠ A K 8 7 6 5 4
♡ J 8
◊ —
♣ J 10 7 5

The ♡K is led. East's hand isn't what West expected, but now declarer can take the ruffing finesse in diamonds against North. And yet he can do better. At trick two he leads the ◊A, discarding the ♡J, and ruffs a diamond. If North follows, the suit can be ruffed out and two club ruffs will suffice. If North shows out, four club ruffs will be needed. That's why it could be fatal to take even one round of trumps. North could have: ♠9 ♡KQ107653 ◊5 ♣K842.

25

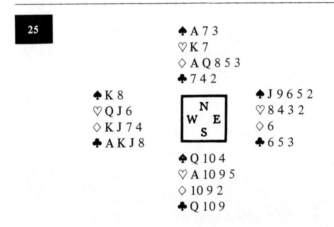

♠ A 7 3
♡ K 7
◊ A Q 8 5 3
♣ 7 4 2

♠ K 8
♡ Q J 6
◊ K J 7 4
♣ A K J 8

♠ J 9 6 5 2
♡ 8 4 3 2
◊ 6
♣ 6 5 3

♠ Q 10 4
♡ A 10 9 5
◊ 10 9 2
♣ Q 10 9

That's a likely layout. You could hardly expect to make more than four tricks in 1NT, and yet they couldn't bid game.

26

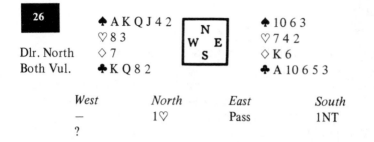

♠ A K Q J 4 2   ♠ 10 6 3
♡ 8 3   ♡ 7 4 2

Dlr. North   ◊ 7   ◊ K 6
Both Vul.   ♣ K Q 8 2   ♣ A 10 6 5 3

West	North	East	South
–	1♡	Pass	1NT
?			

Some Wests may be tempted to double, then to bid spades. That would
show strength, but it would be a short-sighted way of doing it. A jump
to 3♠, to 4♠ at favourable vulnerability, would convey the same
message and make life harder for opponents, who might go a long way
if they found their fit in diamonds. In bidding, as in play, every move
should be focused on the next one — if not on the one after.

27

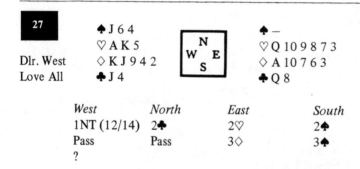

♠ J 6 4   ♠ —
♡ A K 5   ♡ Q 10 9 8 7 3

Dlr. West   ◊ K J 9 4 2   ◊ A 10 7 6 3
Love All   ♣ J 4   ♣ Q 8

West	North	East	South
1NT (12/14)	2♣	2♡	2♠
Pass	Pass	3◊	3♠
?			

You would have passed 2♡, a weakness take-out, but East's 3◊ has
improved your hand beyond measure. You expect to make 5◊, but just
as you have a superb fit, so have they. It's ever thus. Over a *voluntary*
5◊ they may well bid 5♠, and, as likely as not, make it. So bid 4◊,
competitively, then allow yourself to be pushed into 5◊ defensively.

26

Against 4♠ North leads the ♡AK, South following with the ♡10 and ♡Q. A third heart is ruffed and trumps are drawn in two rounds. It looks like eleven tricks, for the ◇7 can be discarded on dummy's fifth club — so long, of course, as the clubs can be brought home without loss. That, then, is the only danger.

Each defender can be disarmed if you know which one has four clubs. The natural play is to start with the ♣K. If South shows out, the finesse is taken against the ♣J.

Since South bid 1NT, however, he cannot have a void. So West starts with the ♣A. If North shows out, he plays the ♣10, covers the ♣J with the ♣Q, goes over to the ♠10 and finesses against the ♣9.

> North: ♠97 ♡AKJ965 ◇Q10852 ♣—
> South: ♠85 ♡Q10 ◇AJ943 ♣J974

27

Suppose that over your 4◇, North bids 4♠ — 'pushing' you into 5◇. After two passes, South doubles. Defenders start with the ♣AK and switch to the ♠K. The only danger is a 3-0 trump break. If so, where's the void?

With South, surely. He wouldn't have doubled with ◇Q85. Too revealing. Moreover, with a void, North might have gone on to 5♠. The hope of a trump trick could make him think differently. The chances are, however, that trumps will break 2-1. Otherwise they wouldn't let you play in 5◇.

> North: ♠KQ7 ♡642 ◇Q ♣AK10763
> South: ♠A1098532 ♡J ◇85 ♣952

Observe that with the perfect fit and the lucky 2-2 club break, 5♠ is unbeatable. Why did South double? The answer is 'on the bidding'. You bid as if you were sacrificing, not as if you expected to make 5◇. Your tactical underbid of 4◇ paid dividends. And you had nothing to lose.

28

Dlr. North
Love All

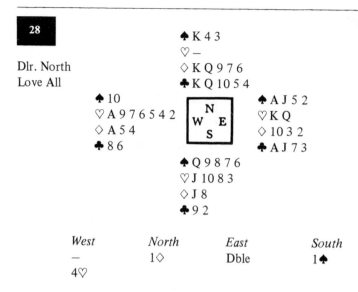

♠ K 4 3
♡ —
◇ K Q 9 7 6
♣ K Q 10 5 4

♠ 10
♡ A 9 7 6 5 4 2
◇ A 5 4
♣ 8 6

N
W   E
S

♠ A J 5 2
♡ K Q
◇ 10 3 2
♣ A J 7 3

♠ Q 9 8 7 6
♡ J 10 8 3
◇ J 8
♣ 9 2

West	North	East	South
—	1◇	Dble	1♠
4♡			

East has nothing to spare for his double, but whatever it is, West is worth 4♡.

North leads the ♣3. West sees ten tricks — until the 4-0 trump break comes to light. Then the total shrinks to nine. By the same token, he has four losers. How can he thwart an unkind destiny? The answer is by taking his ten winners first. All hinges on trick two. Will he, obeying an automatic reflex, take a round of trumps? Then he's lost. Will he, obeying the technician's instinct, ruff a spade? Then the story will have a happy ending. Crossing twice in trumps he will ruff two more spades. Next, he will duck a club and, winning the return, cash the ♣A and ruff a club. It wouldn't help South to ruff in front of him. That's eight tricks without counting the two red aces.

But observe that declarer needs four entries in dummy and cannot afford to waste one of them at trick two by cashing a top trump. Ruffing in this situation, with a superfluity of trumps, should be a habit — like not obeying automatic reflexes.

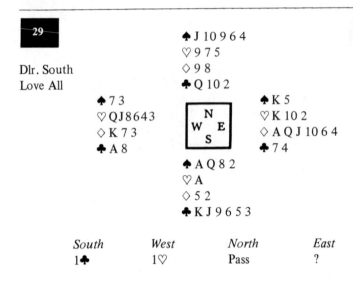

29

Dlr. South
Love All

♠ J 10 9 6 4
♡ 9 7 5
◇ 9 8
♣ Q 10 2

♠ 7 3
♡ Q J 8 6 4 3
◇ K 7 3
♣ A 8

♠ K 5
♡ K 10 2
◇ A Q J 10 6 4
♣ 7 4

♠ A Q 8 2
♡ A
◇ 5 2
♣ K J 9 6 5 3

South	West	North	East
1♣	1♡	Pass	?

Does the book advise 2◇ or, more likely, 3◇? Put it down and bid 4♡. For what would you do if, in response to 2◇, West bid 2♡? Would you raise to 3♡, invitational but no longer forcing? Surely that would be pusillanimous, and if you intend to go to 4♡ anyway, why not do it at once, denying opponents the chance to bid again and discover their spade fit? As the cards are, they can make 4♠ if they get there!

Against 4♡ North leads the ♣2 to South's ♣K. Can you make certain of the contract? Yes, but only if you master the automatic reflex to win the first trick, intending to drive out the ♡A — which South should have on the bidding — and discard a spade, both spades maybe, on the diamonds.

South won't give you the chance. In with the ♡A, he will put North in with a club and take two more tricks after the predestined spade return. So let the ♣K hold, cutting enemy communications, and be safe for ever after.

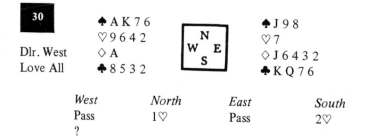

30	♠ A K 7 6		♠ J 9 8
	♡ 9 6 4 2		♡ 7
Dlr. West	◇ A		◇ J 6 4 3 2
Love All	♣ 8 5 3 2		♣ K Q 7 6

West	North	East	South
Pass	1♡	Pass	2♡
?			

A good hand for heretics. An overcall normally promises a 5-card suit —
at the two level a *good* 5-card (or 6-card) suit. Yet here West can
safely come in with 2♠! Consider. East is marked with one heart or
none and surely has at least three spades. At worst West will score
seven or eight tricks on a cross-ruff, but there may easily be a game
in spades on sub-standard values, or maybe a cheap save. Bid 2♠.

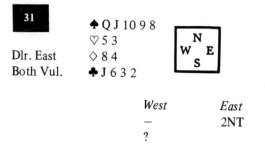

31	♠ Q J 10 9 8	
	♡ 5 3	
Dlr. East	◇ 8 4	
Both Vul.	♣ J 6 3 2	

West	East
—	2NT
?	

If you pass, no one will blame you, but if you don't, be prepared to
play in 4♠. There's nothing else. Should you bid 3♠, partner, with a
doubleton, will rebid 3NT. If he has ♠Kx you will bring him one trick,
and if he has ♠Ax or ♠AK, you will bring him none, for you have
no entry. Let's say that you chance your arm in 4♠.

30

North leads the ♡K and promptly switches to a low trump, dummy's
♠8 winning. West comes to hand with the ◇A and ruffs a heart, ruffs
a diamond, then another heart and another diamond. Having scored
five tricks, he cashes the ♠AK and exits with a club.

> North: ♠Q105 ♡AK105 ◇Q975 ♣A4
> South: ♠432 ♡QJ83 ◇K108 ♣J109

Despite a disappointing dummy and North's good switch to a trump at
trick two, West must come to eight tricks.

There are many situations, such as the above, in which conventional
standards should be drastically modified in the light of information
conveyed by opponents' bidding. For a study of this fascinating subject
I recommend Michael Lawrence's *The Complete Book on Overcalls*.

31

♠ Q J 10 9 8		♠ A 4
♡ 5 3	N	♡ A Q 10
◇ 8 4	W E	◇ A K 7 3 2
♣ J 6 3 2	S	♣ A 8 4

The ♣5 is led. You'll need luck to score ten tricks. Win with the ♣A,
cash the ◇AK and ruff a diamond. Take the heart finesse and ruff
another. Next the ♡A, a heart ruff and a spade to the ♠A, your ninth
trick. Now lead dummy's fifth diamond, hoping to find South with the
♠K. If so, you'll score your last trump *en passant*. This would be a
friendly distribution:

> North: ♠65 ♡K8642 ◇Q10 ♣Q1075
> South: ♠K732 ♡J97 ◇J965 ♣K9

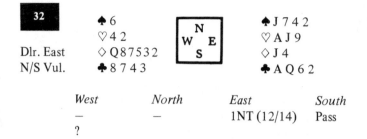

32	♠ 6		♠ J 7 4 2
	♡ 4 2	N	♡ A J 9
Dlr. East	◇ Q 8 7 5 3 2	W E	◇ J 4
N/S Vul.	♣ 8 7 4 3	S	♣ A Q 6 2

West	North	East	South
—	—	1NT (12/14)	Pass
?			

The weak 1NT has many virtues, but when partner has nothing it can be expensive. A favourite ploy, if doubled, is for responder to bid his shortest suit, then to redouble for a rescue. Since responder can pass with 10-11 points, opponents, too, run risks if they step in at the wrong time. Here West passes. North may pass, too, but he doubles, South passes and now West bids 2◇. North doubles again and all pass.

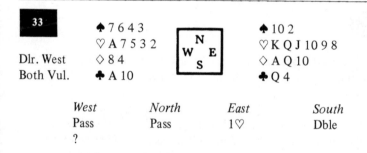

33	♠ 7 6 4 3		♠ 10 2
	♡ A 7 5 3 2	N	♡ K Q J 10 9 8
Dlr. West	◇ 8 4	W E	◇ A Q 10
Both Vul.	♣ A 10	S	♣ Q 4

West	North	East	South
Pass	Pass	1♡	Dble
?			

Had South passed, West would bid 3♡. Over a double any raise is pre-emptive, intended to shut out opponents. Here West would bid 3♡ without the ♣A. Should he now bid 4♡?

With two aces in defence there's no need to stretch, for there's a widely accepted convention to show a genuine jump raise over a double — 2NT. With a minimum opening opener signs off in 3♡. Here he has enough for 4♡.

32

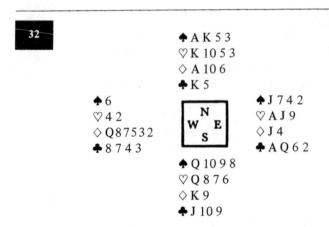

```
            ♠ A K 5 3
            ♡ K 10 5 3
            ◇ A 10 6
            ♣ K 5
♠ 6                        ♠ J 7 4 2
♡ 4 2          N           ♡ A J 9
◇ Q87532    W   E         ◇ J 4
♣ 8 7 4 3       S          ♣ A Q 6 2
            ♠ Q 10 9 8
            ♡ Q 8 7 6
            ◇ K 9
            ♣ J 10 9
```

The ♠K is led. West will ruff three spades, score two clubs and two hearts, the ♡10 being right for him, and remain with ◇Q87 opposite ◇J9. Eight tricks. Lucky? Certainly, but one down would be no tragedy.

33

South leads the ♠K, the ♠A and a third spade to North's queen. East ruffs and lays down the ♡K, both defenders following. How should he continue?

Unless South was stretching unduly he should have both the minor-suit kings for his take-out double and, if so, East can spread his hand. Crossing to the ♡A he ruffs dummy's last spade and exits with the ◇Q. South must lead away from his ♣K or else play into the ◇A10. Alternatively, after the spade ruff, declarer can cash the ♣A and exit with the ♣Q. South will be forced to concede a ruff and discard or else play into the ◇AQ.

North: ♠Q85 ♡4 ◇9765 ♣97653
South: ♠AKJ9 ♡6 ◇KJ32 ♣KJ82

34

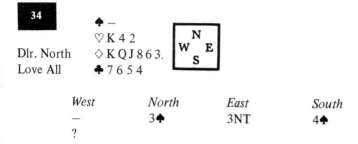

♠ —
♡ K 4 2
Dlr. North   ◇ K Q J 8 6 3.
Love All   ♣ 7 6 5 4

West	North	East	South
–	3♠	3NT	4♠
?			

What must East have to justify his 3NT bid? Presumably, after stopping the spades, he expects to run six or seven clubs and he should have an honour in hearts and the ◇A — or the suit would be wide open. West can, therefore, bid 6◇ or 6♣. Which should it be? Clubs have the edge, for with ten or eleven between the two hands a void is not unlikely and in 6◇ a club ruff, after the ♡A perhaps, is a distinct possibility.

35

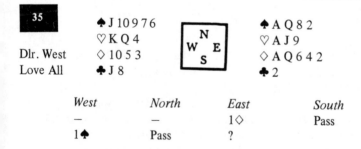

♠ J 10 9 7 6   ♠ A Q 8 2
♡ K Q 4   ♡ A J 9
Dlr. West   ◇ 10 5 3   ◇ A Q 6 4 2
Love All   ♣ J 8   ♣ 2

West	North	East	South
–	–	1◇	Pass
1♠	Pass	?	

A widely used convention, ideal in this situation, is the *splinter bid* — a double jump in a new suit, showing a singleton or void and implying strong support for the last bid suit. The bid here is 4♣.

With a minimum, West signs off in 4♠. Give him the ◇K and the slam would be on a finesse, yet not so easy to reach till West is relieved of worries about his clubs.

```
34        ♠ —              ┌─────┐      ♠ K 9 4
          ♡ K 4 2          │  N  │      ♡ J 6 5
          ◇ K Q J 8 6 3    │W   E│      ◇ A
          ♣ 7 6 5 4        │  S  │      ♣ A K Q J 9 3
                           └─────┘
```

North leads the ♣J, ducked and ruffed by West. On a club at trick two North throws a spade. The diamonds being blocked, how can West draw trumps and get back to his hand? The ♡K? Since North's spades are evidently wretched, he may well have the ♡A.

The answer is to ruff a spade, cross to the ◇A and ruff another. Next, West should lead diamonds, discarding dummy's hearts. So long as South has three or more diamonds he can at best take one trick, a trump.

> North: ♠J1086532 ♡AQ3 ◇542 ♣—
> South: ♠AQ7 ♡10987 ◇1097 ♣1082

```
35
```

North leads the ◇9. He isn't the cunning type, so the ◇KJ are both likely to be wrong. West rises with dummy's ◇A and sees South drop the ◇J. What should he do next?

Declarer appears, at worst, to have three losers — a diamond, a spade and a club — but what if South comes in with the ♠K, cashes the ◇K and, putting North in with a club, ruffs a diamond?

To parry the threat West applies the **scissors coup**. At trick two, before South can ruff anything, West leads a club. When South comes in with the ♠K he can cash the ◇K, but he has no means of putting North in, for the scissors have snipped the cord between their hands.

> North: ♠3 ♡10532 ◇987 ♣AQ1063
> South: ♠K54 ♡876 ◇KJ ♣K9754

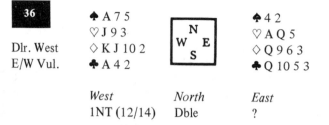

36

Dlr. West
E/W Vul.

♠ A 7 5
♡ J 9 3
◇ K J 10 2
♣ A 4 2

♠ 4 2
♡ A Q 5
◇ Q 9 6 3
♣ Q 10 5 3

West	North	East
1NT (12/14)	Dble	?

The book bid is redouble. But what will happen if you do? Opponents won't stick it. More than half the time one or other will find a 5 or 6-card suit as a refuge. A double will probably bring you 300. If you pass there's a good chance that South will pass too, and with every high card marked, West should make an overtrick — maybe even two. Either is better than 300. So at unfavourable vulnerability, pass. At other times, redouble.

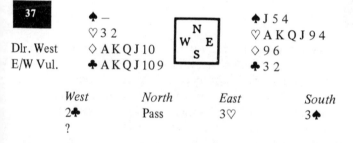

37

Dlr. West
E/W Vul.

♠ —
♡ 3 2
◇ A K Q J 10
♣ A K Q J 10 9

♠ J 5 4
♡ A K Q J 9 4
◇ 9 6
♣ 3 2

West	North	East	South
2♣	Pass	3♡	3♠
?			

A jump over a forcing bid is the accepted method of showing a solid suit. West could, therefore, go straight to 7♡. But there's no rush. At the vulnerability almost any sacrifice would be worthwhile for North-South, so if East has the ♠A — and a solid heart suit doesn't rule it out — 7NT would be the answer. To find out, West should bid 4NT — a very rare case for Blackwood with a void.

36

Against 1NT doubled, North leads the ♠K, ♠Q and ♠J. West wins, finesses the ♡Q and drives out the ◇A. North has two more spades to cash — on which West throws clubs — and exits with a diamond. West plays off his two diamond winners and with ten cards gone — five spades, one heart and four diamonds — one of North's kings, the ♡K or ♣K must be bare. If the ♣K doesn't fall on the ace, the ♡K will, and the ♡J will yield West an overtrick.

> North: ♠KQJ93　♡K104　◇A54　♣K6
> South: ♠1086　♡8762　◇87　♣J987

West could play virtually double-dummy, but that's what East should expect on the bidding.

Observe that if East redoubles and North takes it out into 2♠, he can hardly fail to make six tricks and will make seven if he gets the chance to ruff a diamond.

37

Against 7♡ South leads the ♠K, ruffed in dummy. On the ♡A South shows out. No wonder North wasn't keen on sacrificing!

To catch the unfinessable ♡10 declarer applies the trump reduction technique we met in **8**. He reduces the trumps to North's level, eliminates the side-suits and, with ♡J9 poised over North's ♡108, leads from dummy. This requires adequate entries and correct timing.

A club ruff establishes trump parity. Crossing to the ◇A East then leads clubs till North, with trumps only left, is forced to ruff. Needless to say, it wouldn't help North to ruff earlier, for East would then extract his last trump and get back to dummy with his second diamond.

> North: ♠A63　♡108765　◇53　♣864
> South: ♠KQ109872　♡—　◇8742　♣75

Because the trump reduction is effected by ruffing a winner, this play bears the grandiloquent title of *Grand Coup*.

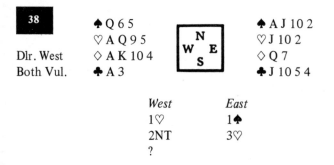

38	♠ Q 6 5		♠ A J 10 2
	♡ A Q 9 5		♡ J 10 2
Dlr. West	◇ A K 10 4		◇ Q 7
Both Vul.	♣ A 3		♣ J 10 5 4

West	East
1♡	1♠
2NT	3♡
?	

With four hearts, East would have raised at once, so he now shows three and suggests 4♡ as an alternative to 3NT. Having only four hearts, West doesn't want to be in game on a 4-3 fit. Should he then bid 3NT? That's the second best bid. It costs nothing to show 3-card support for East by bidding 3♠. With only four spades, East calls 3NT.

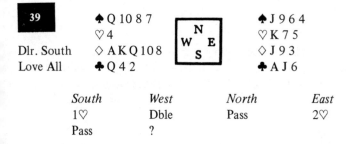

39	♠ Q 10 8 7		♠ J 9 6 4
	♡ 4		♡ K 7 5
Dlr. South	◇ A K Q 10 8		◇ J 9 3
Love All	♣ Q 4 2		♣ A J 6

South	West	North	East
1♡	Dble	Pass	2♡
Pass	?		

West should bid 2♠, not 3◇. East's cue-bid *guarantees* four spades — or a still better hand. East's bid is questionable. To protect his ♡K — and without it he certainly isn't worth 2♡ — he should have bid 2♠, so that the lead should run up to him. In the event, West bid 2♠, East 3♠ and West went on to game.

38

North led the ♣9 to dummy's ♣10, South's ♣Q and West's ♣A. Anxious to keep North out, West began with the spade finesse, losing to South's ♠K. Back came a heart, but that finesse was wrong, too, and the club return sealed declarer's fate, the other hands being:

North: ♠943 ♡K3 ◇J8532 ♣982
South: ♠K87 ♡8764 ◇96 ♣KQ76

Bad luck? On East, certainly. All West had to do was to play low from dummy at trick one. Thereafter he could afford to lose both finesses — and two clubs.

Where, or rather why, did West go wrong? Because instead of counting his losers and winners at trick one, he did 'what comes naturally' — an expensive habit.

39

North led the ♡10, then the ♡9 ruffed by West, who played a trump. South won with the ♠K, cashed the ♠A and continued with a third trump. West reeled off his diamonds, but that only came to eight tricks and the club king, predictably wrong, scored the fourth trick for the defence.

West made the same mistake as on the previous hand. Perhaps it was the same West. Instead of counting his tricks, he played a trump automatically. It was the 'natural' thing to do. Had he counted, he would have crossed to the ◇J and ruffed the ♡K, his tenth trick. Then he would have played a trump.

North: ♠53 ♡10962 ◇765 ♣10753
South: ♠AK2 ♡AQJ83 ◇42 ♣K98

South couldn't force dummy with another heart, for West would still have a trump left.

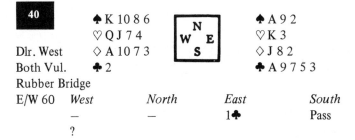

40	♠ K 10 8 6		♠ A 9 2
	♡ Q J 7 4	N	♡ K 3
Dlr. West	◇ A 10 7 3	W E	◇ J 8 2
Both Vul.	♣ 2	S	♣ A 9 7 5 3

Rubber Bridge

E/W 60	*West*	*North*	*East*	*South*
	—	—	1♣	Pass
	?			

Without the part-score the correct response is 1◇, allowing maximum room to find a fit in any one of three suits. At rubber bridge, with 60 up, I advocate rank heresy. Bid 1NT, the worst bid without the partial. No longer need you look for a fit. You should be able to convert without one and you force opponents, if they try to save the rubber, to come in at the two level. A vicious double awaits them.

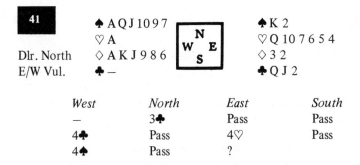

41	♠ A Q J 10 9 7		♠ K 2
	♡ A	N	♡ Q 10 7 6 5 4
Dlr. North	◇ A K J 9 8 6	W E	◇ 3 2
E/W Vul.	♣ —	S	♣ Q J 2

	West	*North*	*East*	*South*
	—	3♣	Pass	Pass
	4♣	Pass	4♡	Pass
	4♠	Pass	?	

To pass or not to pass? West has shown a puissant hand but no interest in hearts. What do you bring him? The ♠K, of course, and the doubleton diamond may be useful too. With a diamond honour, instead of the useless ♣QJ, you would certainly encourage. Now it's close, but West was too good to bid 4♠ directly, so there should be enough for 5♠. After all, West can pass.

40

Compare the results of the hand played by West and East respectively, in 1NT, the likely contract if West correctly responds 1◇. The other hands could be:

> North: ♠J75 ♡865 ◇K964 ♣K108
> South: ♠Q43 ♡A1092 ◇Q5 ♣QJ64

With the West hand concealed from view, declarer may well come to eight tricks, maybe even nine if defenders don't switch to clubs in time. Played by East the contract itself cannot be guaranteed and, with the West hand exposed, an early switch to clubs is a certainty.

This doesn't prove that, other things being equal, the 'bad' response of 1NT is better than the 'good' one of 1◇. But other things aren't always equal and the surprise element in a 'bad' bid might make the play a lot easier.

41

Against 6♠ North leads the ♡J, clearly a singleton. The trumps are solid, so declarer's thoughts are on the diamonds. If they are 3-2 there's no problem, and if they are 5-0 there's no hope, so the focus is on a 4-1 break when, if a top diamond is ruffed, another diamond loser will be unavoidable. West visualises this sort of layout:

> North: ♠3 ♡J ◇Q1075 ♣K1076543
> South: ♠8654 ♡K9832 ◇4 ♣A98

To make sure of losing one diamond only he lays down the ◇A and leads a low diamond. Whatever the return, he will ruff a diamond with the ♠K and live happily ever after.

Note how lethal a trump lead would be. At trick three, South would ruff North's diamond winner and return a trump, killing the ruff — and the contract.

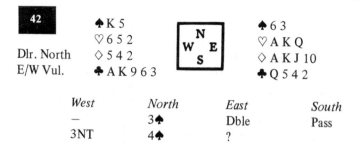

42	♠ K 5		♠ 6 3
	♡ 6 5 2		♡ A K Q
Dlr. North	♢ 5 4 2		♢ A K J 10
E/W Vul.	♣ A K 9 6 3		♣ Q 5 4 2

West	North	East	South
–	3♠	Dble	Pass
3NT	4♠	?	

Pass. Partner must know more about your hand than you do about his. Needless to say, it's a *forcing pass*. North doesn't expect to make 4♠ — he wouldn't have opened 3♠ if he did — and you could double confidently, but you don't want to prejudice West. Here he could bid 4NT, but will probably feel safer in 5♣.

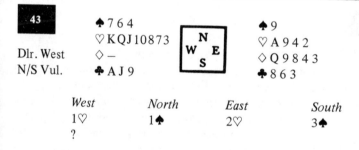

43	♠ 7 6 4		♠ 9
	♡ K Q J 10 8 7 3		♡ A 9 4 2
Dlr. West	♢ –		♢ Q 9 8 4 3
N/S Vul.	♣ A J 9		♣ 8 6 3

West	North	East	South
1♡	1♠	2♡	3♠
?			

You have more than enough to bid 4♡, but whatever you do opponents will surely bid 4♠ and, if you go on to 5♡, they may well bid 5♠. Then, instead of playing in 5♡ and hoping to make it, you will be driven to 6♡ — expecting to go down, or defending 5♠ — not knowing what will happen.

Pass. Wait for the inevitable 4♠, then 'sacrifice' gallantly. Now you may well be doubled.

42

North leads the ♡J against 5♣.

Trumps have priority and here the danger is a 4-0 break, by no means unlikely on North's bidding. If he has a void, however, South's ♣J1087 can be picked up, so long as declarer starts with the ♣Q. When North shows out, the ♣9 is finessed, unless South splits his honours. If he does, West wins, crosses to the ♣A and repeats the finesse.

Now only the diamond position remains to be cleared up. West must not finesse. If North has the ◇Q, the finesse isn't needed. Let North make the trick. He can do no harm. If South wins the trick a spade from him would be lethal, so West should give himself the chance of a doubleton ◇Q. It costs nothing to play for the drop and wins the day if the hands are:

> North: ♠AQJ10742 ♡J10 ◇9763 ♣—
> South: ♠98 ♡98743 ◇Q8 ♣J1087

43

Against 5♡ doubled North leads the ♠A, then the ◇K.

At first sight the contract seems to depend on finding the club honours favourably divided, but the diamond switch creates an option. If the suit splits 4-4 you have enough entries in dummy to ruff it out. Alternatively, the ◇A may come down. After ruffing the ◇K, ruff a spade, another diamond, another spade and a third diamond. If nothing happens and you think that North started with five diamonds, two trump entries remain to finesse in clubs. South's card at trick two, on the ◇K, should give you a pretty good idea of the position. At this early stage he will surely signal his count correctly to his partner, high-low with two or four. And of course, you will be watching him like a hawk.

> North: ♠AJ532 ♡6 ◇AK105 ♣K102
> South: ♠KQ108 ♡5 ◇J762 ♣Q754

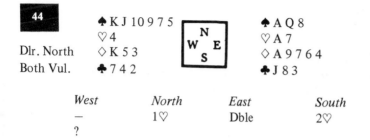

44			

Dlr. North
Both Vul.

♠ K J 10 9 7 5
♡ 4
◇ K 5 3
♣ 7 4 2

♠ A Q 8
♡ A 7
◇ A 9 7 6 4
♣ J 8 3

West	*North*	*East*	*South*
—	1♡	Dble	2♡
?			

If in doubt between 3♠ and 4♠, bid 4♠ without flinching. Unless, for tactical reasons, you want to be 'pushed', go all the way at once, putting maximum pressure on opponents.

Here you have four losers, but East could just as easily have two clubs and a third heart, making 4♠ a certainty. When in doubt, bid one more.

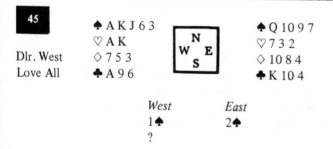

45			

Dlr. West
Love All

♠ A K J 6 3
♡ A K
◇ 7 5 3
♣ A 9 6

♠ Q 10 9 7
♡ 7 3 2
◇ 10 8 4
♣ K 10 4

West	*East*
1♠	2♠
?	

West has enough to bid 4♠, but there's no hurry and a little judicious hocus-pocus may improve his chances. It costs nothing to bid 3◇ on the way round, seemingly a trial bid. It may put off North from leading the suit. But don't try this too often against the same defenders. Next time make an 'inhibitory' bid, as it is known, in a suit you want 'led'. Vary your tactics.

44

North leads the ♡K.

There's no way of making ten tricks against a double-dummy defence, but that is something you will not always get, which is why measured optimism is justified in the bidding.

You start with a considerable advantage. You can see three club losers. Defenders can't. With ♣AK North would have probably led the ♣K, if only to look at dummy. So his club holding is likely to be different. Let him hold the first trick. Unless he switches to a club, which is far from certain, you will throw a diamond on the ♡A, cash the ◇AK and ruff a diamond, setting up two diamonds for club discards. All you need is a 3-2 diamond break and a not improbable distribution, such as:

> North: ♠42 ♡KQJ103 ◇Q82 ♣AQ9
> South: ♠63 ♡98652 ◇J10 ♣K1065

45

Against 4♠ North leads the ♠5. After drawing trumps in two rounds declarer cashes the ♡AK, crosses in trumps, ruffs dummy's third heart and exits with a diamond. Defenders can take three diamonds, but must then present declarer with a ruff and discard or else open up the clubs. Playing for split honours, West will have a good chance of making his contract.

Observe that had the defence started with diamonds West would have had to tackle the clubs himself and, short of finding the ♣QJ bare, he would have surely gone down.

> North: ♠52 ♡Q1084 ◇QJ2 ♣Q732
> South: ♠84 ♡J965 ◇AK96 ♣J85

Without the inhibitory bid would North have led the ◇Q? No one can tell, but West did well to discourage him.

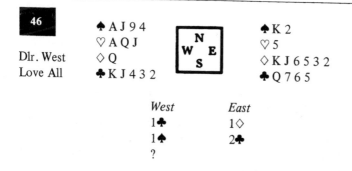

46	♠ A J 9 4	♠ K 2
	♡ A Q J	♡ 5
Dlr. West	◇ Q	◇ K J 6 5 3 2
Love All	♣ K J 4 3 2	♣ Q 7 6 5

West	East
1♣	1◇
1♠	2♣
?	

You have enough for 3NT, but 2NT may be best. The clubs are diaphanous and the singleton ◇Q isn't much help. East, evidently a conservative bidder, must have been sorely tempted to call 3♣ over 1♠, and were the suit a major, he would have surely done so. Presumably he feared that 3♣ would lead to 3NT and this he didn't fancy. He is happy, of course, to raise 2NT to game.

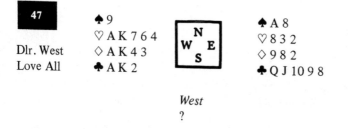

47	♠ 9	♠ A 8
	♡ A K 7 6 4	♡ 8 3 2
Dlr. West	◇ A K 4 3	◇ 9 8 2
Love All	♣ A K 2	♣ Q J 10 9 8

West
?

The singleton spade precludes 2NT, while the hearts aren't good enough for any sort of 2♡ bid. So West opens 1♡ and jumps to 3◇ over the 1NT response. East can only revert to 3♡ and it needs courage for West to try again with 4♣. If he does, 4♠ will spur him on to a slam, but will he venture 4♣?

A good hand for 1♣ systems.

46

Against 3NT North leads the ♡6 to South's ♡9 and your ♡Q. How should you play?

Setting up the clubs will ensure eight tricks, so long as they split no worse than 3-1. So you need one more. If you had another diamond you could leave the clubs alone and get home with five tricks in diamonds, assuming a 3-2 break. Pretend to have another diamond. Cross to the ♠K and lead the ◊2. If North has the ◊A he can do no harm. If South has it, not knowing that your ◊Q is bare, he will surely play low and you can switch to clubs. The other hands might well be:

> North: ♠Q108 ♡K108643 ◊87 ♣109
> South: ♠8765 ♡972 ◊A1094 ♣A8

47

North leads the ♠K against 4♡. Since it seems to be so easy, West looks for snags and notably for a 4-1 heart break. So he begins by ducking a round of trumps. Forced, with a spade, he again plays low trumps from both hands. Dummy still has a trump, so he cannot be forced again. He is safe.

That is the way to play in a match or at rubber bridge. Paradoxically, the same play is correct in a pairs event, but for a very different reason. No longer is West paying an insurance premium on his contract. He can see that ten tricks are cold in no-trumps, and a slam in hearts is there unless trumps break badly. At IMPs he fears the bad break. At matchpoints it's his best hope.

48

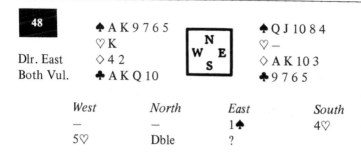

♠ A K 9 7 6 5   ♠ Q J 10 8 4
♡ K   ♡ –
Dlr. East   ◇ 4 2   ◇ A K 10 3
Both Vul.   ♣ A K Q 10   ♣ 9 7 6 5

West	North	East	South
—	—	1♠	4♡
5♡	Dble	?	

Redouble. With powerful trump support, that is the conventional method of showing first-round control over the double of a cue-bid. A pass would indicate second-round control, while with two or more heart losers East would bid 5♠. Over the redouble West would bid 6♣ and East 6◇, and now the stage would be set for 7♠.

49

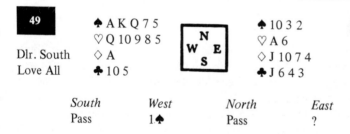

♠ A K Q 7 5   ♠ 10 3 2
♡ Q 10 9 8 5   ♡ A 6
Dlr. South   ◇ A   ◇ J 10 7 4
Love All   ♣ 10 5   ♣ J 6 4 3

South	West	North	East
Pass	1♠	Pass	?

A raise to 2♠ has a two-fold advantage over 1NT. If East doesn't show his modest fit at once he is unlikely to get another chance. Better still, 2♠ has a pre-emptive value. Opponents may come in at the two-level, yet hesitate to bid at the level of three. Certainly, West need only have four spades, for we are not playing 5-card majors, but *in practice* a bid of 1♡ or 1♠ is usually based on a 5-card suit, especially when playing a weak no-trump.

48

South leads the ♡A. East counts thirteen tricks with six trumps, a heart ruff, four clubs and the ◇AK. As he draws trumps, North, with a void, throws two hearts. Next come the ♣AK. The second time South discards a heart. Unlucky. The thirteenth trick has vanished. Can it be replaced? A double finesse in diamonds? A third-round ruff, hoping to drop the ◇QJ?

There's no need to back outsiders, when you can put your money on a real 'cert'. To leap vulnerable to 4♡ without the king, South must surely have eight hearts. He has followed twice in spades and once in clubs, so he cannot have more than two diamonds. North must, therefore, guard both minors. When dummy's last winner is played the remaining three cards will be ◇42 ♣10, facing ◇AK10. And North?

Having started with ♠— ♡9863 ◇J9765 ♣J843, he will have been inexorably squeezed in the minors.

49

North leads the ♣9 against 4♠. South wins with the ♣Q and continues with the ♣K and ♣A. West ruffs and draws trumps, finding South with J94. All hinges on the hearts. Both defenders follow low to the ♡A and ♡6. Which card should West play?

If hearts split 3-3 it's a guess. If they are 4-2, the ♡Q will gain over the ♡10 for North could have a doubleton ♡J. A doubleton ♡K wouldn't help since Jxxx would still take a trick, and taking hearts in isolation, the ♡Q is the right card. But no suit can be divorced from the others. Having shown ♣AKQ ♠J, South, who passed as dealer, cannot have the ♡K, so here the ♡10 would be the right card. But West would do better still to start with the ♡Q from hand. This will restrict his losers to one, if hearts break 3-3 or 4-2 with either defender holding a doubleton honour, as here:

North: ♠86 ♡K4 ◇KQ532 ♣9872
South: ♠J94 ♡J732 ◇986 ♣AKQ

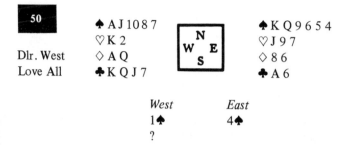

	50
Dlr. West	♠ A J 10 8 7
Love All	♡ K 2
	◇ A Q
	♣ K Q J 7

♠ K Q 9 6 5 4
♡ J 9 7
◇ 8 6
♣ A 6

West	East
1♠	4♠
?	

4NT. Glaringly obvious, but then this is the *right* time for Blackwood.

Here, if East's raise is distributional, he could be aceless. It is possible, so West checks. Use Blackwood to keep out of bad slams, not to get into good ones.

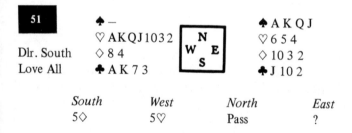

	51
	♠ —
Dlr. South	♡ A K Q J 10 3 2
Love All	◇ 8 4
	♣ A K 7 3

♠ A K Q J
♡ 6 5 4
◇ 10 3 2
♣ J 10 2

South	West	North	East
5◇	5♡	Pass	?

Crediting South with eight diamonds, East doesn't expect West to have more than one, while if he has two, North won't have a diamond to lead. An obvious danger, with freak distributions about, is that a seemingly solid trump suit may spring a leak, and of course West, under pressure, may have stretched. But we are in a buoyant mood, so let's bid 6♡.

50

North leads the ♣10 against 6♠. So long as the ♡A or the ◇K is well placed, all will be well. It looks like an even-money chance. Can declarer do better than guess? And what should he discard from dummy on his long clubs?

The key to the first question lies in the answer to the second. West throws two hearts, crosses and leads the ♡J. If South rises with the ♡A dummy's diamond loser disappears. If he plays the ♡Q and North takes the king with the ace, defenders cannot cash another heart, so West will have time for the diamond finesse. That's a 3-1 on proposition instead of 50-50.

51

North leads the ♡9, South throwing a diamond. Obviously North has no diamond. The void in spades is something East couldn't have foreseen, but unless declarer can get to dummy in time, he will lose two diamonds, to say nothing of a club. A doubleton ♣Q is a possibility, but no more. West, however, needn't look for outside chances. He can make *certain* of the contract for he has a priceless card, the ♡2, which makes up for lack of communications. After the ♡AK, West exits with the ♡2. Whichever black card North returns, West has his entry to dummy. A likely distribution would be:

North: ♠1065432 ♡987 ◇− ♣Q965
South: ♠987 ♡− ◇AKQJ9765 ♣84

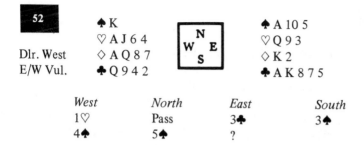

52	♠ K		♠ A 10 5

♠ K
♡ A J 6 4
◊ A Q 8 7
♣ Q 9 4 2

♠ A 10 5
♡ Q 9 3
◊ K 2
♣ A K 8 7 5

Dlr. West
E/W Vul.

West	North	East	South
1♡	Pass	3♣	3♠
4♠	5♠	?	

With IMPs scoring, as was the case here, you lose 17 if you go down in a vulnerable grand slam and you gain 13 if you make it, so you take greater risks than at rubber bridge.

Exchange West's ♠K for the ♡K and there'd be no problem but, at the best of times, duplication of values is an unavoidable hazard, so East bids 7♣.

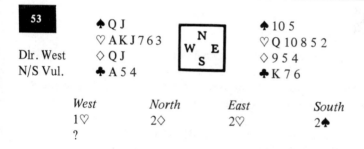

53	♠ Q J		♠ 10 5

♠ Q J
♡ A K J 7 6 3
◊ Q J
♣ A 5 4

♠ 10 5
♡ Q 10 8 5 2
◊ 9 5 4
♣ K 7 6

Dlr. West
N/S Vul.

West	North	East	South
1♡	2◊	2♡	2♠
?			

With an 18 count and a fit for his 6-card suit, West has more than enough, it seems, to bid 4♡, and yet he may not even make 3♡, for there's no worse holding than Qx in the enemy suit(s), except QJ. Those 6 points are a liability. To opponents they would be assets and to make up for them they are likely to have something in clubs, where East has a weak spot. Bid 3♡ competitively.

South led the ♣6. Michael Wolach, declarer when this hand came up, began with the ♣Q, the routine play to guard against a 4-0 trump break.

The slam appeared to depend on the heart finesse, but Wolach was convinced that North had the ♡K. Why? Because at the vulnerability almost any sacrifice, even ten down, would show a profit. If North didn't bid 7♠, it could only be because he had hopes of beating 7♣ and only the ♡K, over the opening 1♡, could inspire such hopes.

After drawing trumps in three rounds, Wolach cashed the ♠A, ruffed a spade and laid down the ♡A, the key play. Now he cashed his last three trumps, remaining with ♡Q9 ◇K2, and leaving dummy with ◇AQ87.

Having started with ♠987 ♡K10752 ◇J1094 ♣3, North was inexorably squeezed.

A perfect *Vienna Coup*, but without the psychological insight the best technique would have been of no avail.

There is no way of making 3♡ against double-dummy defence but that, as we have already noted, isn't always forthcoming. Let's say that North lays down the ◇K and, seeing South's ◇2, switches to the ♠K and ♠2. Winning with the ♠A, South returns the ◇7 to North's ◇A.

<blockquote>
North: ♠K2 ♡4 ◇AK1086 ♣QJ1093
South: ♠A987643 ♡9 ◇732 ♣82
</blockquote>

The importance of continuing with the ◇10 may not be apparent to North. Suppose that he switches to the ♣Q. Turn to South. He has shown three diamonds and clearly six spades. If he has a heart he can only have two clubs, and if so, North must guard both minors.

Winning the club switch in hand, West leads out his trumps. On the last one North must discard from ◇10 ♣J9, while dummy, over him, retains ◇9 ♣K7. North is squeezed. Oh, why didn't he play the ◇10?

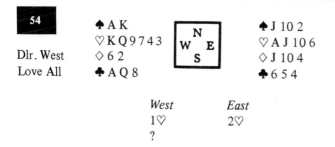

	54	♠ A K		♠ J 10 2
		♡ K Q 9 7 4 3		♡ A J 10 6
Dlr. West		◇ 6 2		◇ J 10 4
Love All		♣ A Q 8		♣ 6 5 4

West	East
1♡	2♡
?	

West has ample values to go straight to 4♡, but as we saw recently **(45)**, a little hocus-pocus can do no harm. Any lead would be more helpful than a diamond, so maybe a fake 'trial' bid of 3◇ would deter it. But perhaps we've executed that manoeuvre recently against the present North. Then let's try 3♣. If he suspects us of fearing clubs he may lead one.

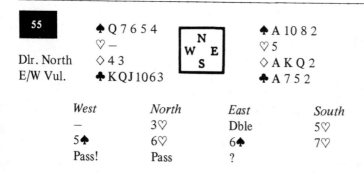

	55	♠ Q 7 6 5 4		♠ A 10 8 2
		♡ –		♡ 5
Dlr. North		◇ 4 3		◇ A K Q 2
E/W Vul.		♣ K Q J 10 6 3		♣ A 7 5 2

West	North	East	South
–	3♡	Dble	5♡
5♠	6♡	6♠	7♡
Pass!	Pass	?	

West's *forcing pass* is significant. With a heart loser he would have surely doubled as a warning to East. Clearly, West is prepared to take a chance in a grand slam, worth three or four times as much as the likely penalty. Bold bidding by West? True, but East's double guarantees spade support and West's clubs will provide all the required winners. East bids 7♠.

54

Defender's begin with the ♢AKQ. West ruffs.

As the beginner sees it, the contract hinges on the club finesse, so he takes it stoically. Even-money. A more seasoned practitioner first cashes the ♠AK, in case the ♠Q drops. A still more experienced player eliminates. After one round of trumps, he cashes the ♠AK, goes over to the ♡A and ruffs the ♠J. Back in dummy with a third trump he leads a club and, if South plays low, inserts the ♣8. Not every South would go up with the ♣J, as he should do from, say, ♣J732, and if he doesn't, declarer is home whoever has the ♣K.

It's better than the other plays, and yet West can double his chances. Instead of ruffing the ♠J, he discards the ♣8, a loser-on-loser, end-playing North. If South has the ♣Q, West ruffs and exits with the ♣8. He still makes his contract if South has the ♣K.

55

North leads the ♡K. The trump position is depressing, each player having placed partner with something better. What should West pray for? A bare ♠K with North? No good, for South would then have ♠J93, a certain trick. The only hope is to pin a singleton ♠J with South. So, ruffing the ♡K, West leads the ♠Q. North covers, and on the ♠A South duly drops the ♠J. West sighs with relief. All he need now do is to get back and finesse against North's ♠93. Simple. Yes, but how should he get back? North is pretty well marked with ten cards in the majors. Has he two diamonds and one club or three diamonds and no club?

I would hate to be in West's shoes.

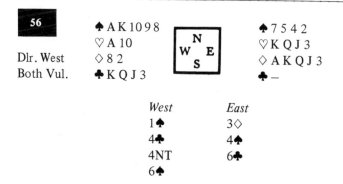

56	♠ A K 10 9 8		♠ 7 5 4 2
	♡ A 10		♡ K Q J 3
Dlr. West	◇ 8 2		◇ A K Q J 3
Both Vul.	♣ K Q J 3		♣ —

West	East
1♠	3◇
4♣	4♠
4NT	6♣
6♠	

East's response of 6♣ over 4NT, to indicate one ace and a void in clubs, is only one of the methods of showing a void in response to Blackwood. Another is to make the normal response but at the six level, showing aces and an unspecified void. It matters little which method you follow — so long as it's the same as partner's!

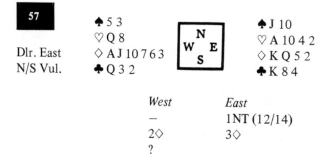

57	♠ 5 3		♠ J 10
	♡ Q 8		♡ A 10 4 2
Dlr. East	◇ A J 10 7 6 3		◇ K Q 5 2
N/S Vul.	♣ Q 3 2		♣ K 8 4

West	East
—	1NT (12/14)
2◇	3◇
?	

Pass quickly. East hasn't discovered another ace and by bidding 3◇ shows weakness, not strength. His purpose is clearly to raise a barrage against South, who might be tempted to balance over 2◇. He is less likely to do it at the three level. Though East-West have a modest preponderance in points, the hand almost certainly belongs to opponents. In defence, 10 points in diamonds will largely be wasted.

56

North leads the ♡9, South following with the ♡2. West wins with the ♡10, ruffs a club and leads a spade. South throws a club.

Is all lost? By no means. West wins with the ♠A, reduces his trumps to North's level, eliminates the side-suits and throws North in with one honour, forcing him to lead away from the other. After the ♠A, West ruffs a club, comes back to the ♡A and ruffs another. The fourth club goes on the ♡K. Next he cashes the ◇AK. Should he now ruff a heart or a diamond? If North over-ruffs, it will be fatal, for his remaining red card will provide a safe exit.

South's ♡2 at trick one is a clue. He had no reason to false card, so he should have an odd number, clearly three, leaving four for North, whose last four cards will be: ♠QJ6 ♡8. West ruffs dummy's last heart and from ♠K109 leads the ♠10 into North's ♠QJ6.

57

North leads the ♠K and switches to a trump, South following.

West's best chance is to set up a trick in hearts, for a club discard. Winning the second round of trumps in dummy he leads the ♡2. If South has the ♡K it's all over. If North captures the ♡Q, West will have a second chance. Other things being equal, he will finesse the ♡10. If they are not, he may have a hunch and play to drop the ♡J in three rounds. The distribution could be:

North: ♠AK76 ♡J976 ◇8 ♣10965
South: ♠Q9842 ♡K53 ◇94 ♣AJ7

Here West makes 3◇, but more important, North-South can make a lucky 4♠, and though they may not bid it, they will doubtless buy the contract if East passes 2◇.

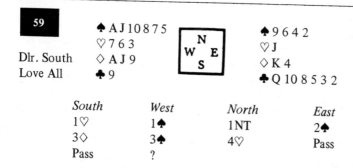

58

Dlr. East
Both Vul.

♠ 6 5 3 2
♡ A Q 10 8 6 4
◇ 6
♣ 3 2

♠ A J 7
♡ —
◇ A K J 7 5
♣ A 10 9 8 7

West	North	East	South
—	—	1◇	Pass
1♡	Pass	2♣	Pass
2♡	Pass	?	

Had you found a fit, you would soon be looking for a slam. But what can you do with a tiresome partner who insists on hearts? The beginner bids 2NT, not realising how hard it is to make tricks when you have no communications with dummy. The optimist bids 3♣, but the best call is — Pass. On misfits pass as soon as possible, preferably sooner. Don't wait to be doubled.

59

Dlr. South
Love All

♠ A J 10 8 7 5
♡ 7 6 3
◇ A J 9
♣ 9

♠ 9 6 4 2
♡ J
◇ K 4
♣ Q 10 8 5 3 2

South	West	North	East
1♡	1♠	1NT	2♠
3◇	3♠	4♡	Pass
Pass	?		

Saving a game which opponents wouldn't make is a costly business. The reverse, or phantom sacrifice by the enemy, is highly desirable. Which is it here? You expect a trick in defence from partner, but no more. In 4♠ you should make eight tricks, probably nine. Should you sacrifice? It's close, but one factor tilts the balance — the chance of pushing the enemy overboard. Bid 4♠. North doubles.

58

Against 2♡ North leads the ♣K. West ducks, wins the next club and ruffs a club, seeing South show out. The ◇AK follow, then another club ruff in the knowledge that North won't over-ruff. Next the ♠A and a diamond ruff. That comes to seven tricks, leaving West with ♠65 ♡AQ10. He will be unlucky not to make nine tricks.

> North: ♠K8 ♡KJ92 ◇932 ♣KQJ5
> South: ♠Q1094 ♡753 ◇Q1084 ♣64

Observe how badly the hand would play in no-trumps. East might end up ignominiously with four tricks and is unlikely to make more than five. East's tops, worth four tricks in no-trumps, bring four more in hearts, serving as entries which allow West to score his trumps by ruffing losers.

59

North leads the ♡10. South wins with the ♡K and continues with the ♡A. North's 1NT and subsequent double point to a 3-0 trump break, so there appear to be four losers — a heart, a club and two trumps. A variation on the trump reduction theme (as in **56**) may dispose of one of them. West shortens his trumps three times; then, when he and North have three cards each and no other cards remain, North is thrown in with one honour and forced to lead away from the other. To succeed this requires a favourable distribution, such as:

> North: ♠KQ3 ♡1095 ◇1076 ♣K764
> South: ♠ − ♡AKQ842 ◇Q8532 ♣AJ

West ruffs the ♡A and concedes a club. If a diamond comes back West wins in dummy, ruffs a club and, crossing with a heart ruff and then a diamond ruff, ruffs two more. This leaves him with ♠AJ10 under North's ♠KQ3. The ♠J seals North's fate.

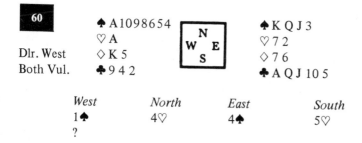

	60	

♠ A 10 9 8 6 5 4
♡ A
Dlr. West   ◇ K 5
Both Vul.   ♣ 9 4 2

♠ K Q J 3
♡ 7 2
◇ 7 6
♣ A Q J 10 5

West	North	East	South
1♠	4♡	4♠	5♡
?			

It's unlikely that they can make 5♡, though with distributional hands one never knows. The same applies to a spade contract. East's hand is a bit of a mystery for he was under pressure. He is, therefore, in the best position to decide what to do. West should make a *forcing pass*. If his hand were markedly unsuitable for 5♠ he would double. Now East must choose. He bids 5♠.

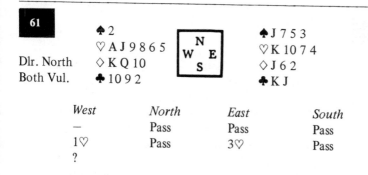

	61	

♠ 2
♡ A J 9 8 6 5
Dlr. North   ◇ K Q 10
Both Vul.   ♣ 10 9 2

♠ J 7 5 3
♡ K 10 7 4
◇ J 6 2
♣ K J

West	North	East	South
–	Pass	Pass	Pass
1♡	Pass	3♡	Pass
?			

It wouldn't be wrong to pass, yet it could be right to bid 4♡. If partner has wasted values in spades, even 3♡ may go down, but give him a useful holding in clubs and 4♡ will probably succeed. It's close, but two factors favour declarer. The bidding has given nothing away and there's next to no risk of a double, so we'll bid 4♡.

60

North leads the ♡K. Unless both the ♣K and ◇A are wrong, the contract is unbeatable. But what if they are? With this in mind West should take the club finesse at once, at trick two. If it fails and South returns a heart, as well he may, the ◇K5 will be parked on the clubs and West will make the rest.

Wouldn't it be safer to take a round of trumps first? It could be fatal. Having none, North, who knows that declarer is unlikely to have a second heart, would signal in diamonds. He mustn't be given the chance.

North: ♠ — ♡KQ108543 ◇AQ84 ♣63
South: ♠72 ♡J96 ◇J10932 ♣K87

It's true that a sophisticated South might be suspicious and return a diamond anyway. Maybe, but give him the chance to go wrong.

61

North leads the ♠K and ♠Q, South following with the ♠6 and ♠4. The contract appears to depend on a guess in clubs, but declarer should be pretty certain of making the right one. The ♡A and ♡K draw trumps in two rounds, South's cards being the ♡Q and ♡2. Now comes the key play — the ♠J. If South has the ♠A he will surely cover, for how could it help him to do otherwise? West ruffs either way and turns to diamonds. His purpose isn't to set up two diamond tricks — there's no hurry about that — but to find out who has the ace. South? Then, if he had the ♠A, he cannot have the ♣A too, for with a 14 count he wouldn't have passed. North is presumed to have the ♠A? Then he can't have the ♣A, for with ♠AKQ and an ace he would have opened the bidding. West plays accordingly.

This is known as *discovery play*.

62

	♠ A 10 5 2	♠ K Q J 6
	♡ 7	♡ A K Q J 10
Dlr. East	◇ A K 6	◇ J 5 2
Both Vul.	♣ J 10 8 5 2	♣ 6

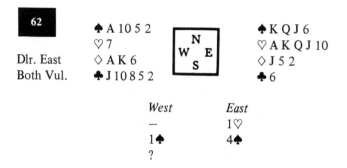

West	East
—	1♡
1♠	4♠
?	

Sensing a slam, West cue-bid his ◇A, and with his second-round control in clubs, East was only too happy to bid 6♠. Reverse West's minors and over 5♣ East would have signed off in 5♠.

This would be a good hand for the splinter bid (see **35**). Over the 1♠ response East would jump to 4♣, showing a powerful spade fit and a control in clubs.

63

	♠ Q 10 8 7 6 5 4 2
	♡ 7 3
Dlr. West	◇ 5 2
N/S Vul.	♣ 4

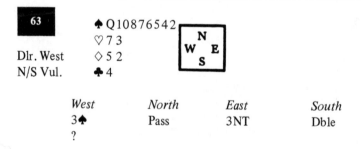

West	North	East	South
3♠	Pass	3NT	Dble
?			

West should have no problem — and above all, no temptation to call 4♠. East knows that he has a long broken suit and nothing much else. West, for his part, cannot place a single card in East's hand. With outside stoppers, and ♠AKx, he may be relying on a lot of spade tricks. Conversely, he may have nine or ten tricks of his own and no spades. The double makes no difference.

62

North led a trump. West took a second round, South throwing a heart. With eleven top tricks declarer looked to a club ruff for his twelfth. So at trick three he played the ♣J. North won and made the deadly return of a heart, killing a vital link with dummy. Now if West ruffed a club he couldn't draw all the trumps and get back to dummy, and when the ◇Q failed to drop, he conceded defeat.

He shouldn't have given in so easily. Instead of a club ruff in dummy he should have cashed the ◇AK, thrown a diamond on a heart and ruffed the ◇J in his hand. Now he could draw the rest of the trumps from dummy.

North: ♠9742 ♡65 ◇Q94 ♣AQ94
South: ♠8 ♡98432 ◇10873 ♣K73

This hand is featured in *Dentro Il Bridge Con Belladonna*.

63

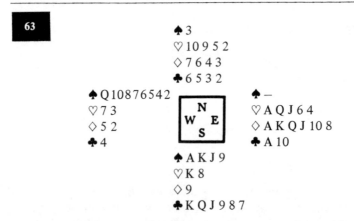

♠ 3
♡ 10 9 5 2
◇ 7 6 4 3
♣ 6 5 3 2

♠ Q 10 8 7 6 5 4 2
♡ 7 3
◇ 5 2
♣ 4

N
W E
S

♠ —
♡ A Q J 6 4
◇ A K Q J 10 8
♣ A 10

♠ A K J 9
♡ K 8
◇ 9
♣ K Q J 9 8 7

Against 3NT South leads the ♣K. East wins and reels off his diamonds, then exits with the ♣10. Unless South has bared his ♡K — the discards will be indicative — his last two cards will be ♡K8. Note that declarer must win the first trick to retain the ♣10, the throw-in card.

64

♠ 9 8 2		♠ J 4 3
♡ A K 7 6 4 3		♡ 10 8 5 2
◇ 4 3		◇ A Q 8
♣ A 8		♣ Q J 10

Dlr. East
Love All

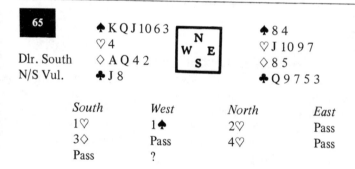

West	North	East	South
—	—	Pass	Pass
1♡	Pass	2♡	Pass
3♡	Pass	?	

East, clearly a very conservative player, has a super-maximum for his raise to 2♡. What should he do now? 4♡? 3NT? The answer is: a serene pass. Had West intended a *trial* bid he could have chosen any one of three suits. His 3♡ shows weakness in defence, not strength in attack. He wants to deter opponents from balancing (see **57**). Had East bid 3♡ before, West would have passed. Now East should pass.

65

♠ K Q J 10 6 3		♠ 8 4
♡ 4		♡ J 10 9 7
◇ A Q 4 2		◇ 8 5
♣ J 8		♣ Q 9 7 5 3

Dlr. South
N/S Vul.

South	West	North	East
1♡	1♠	2♡	Pass
3◇	Pass	4♡	Pass
Pass	?		

With one heart loser only and the ◇AQ well placed, West saw 4♠ as a well-judged sacrifice. Both attractions should have warned him *against* sacrificing. The ◇AQ promised two tricks in defence. The singleton heart pointed to a bad trump break — in short, an unlucky hand for declarer — the very time not to sacrifice. The East hand is just about the useless sort of dummy West should have expected.

64

Defenders take three spades, then North switches to the ♡Q. South shows out. Can West make 3♡ if both minor kings are wrong? If North has both?

The position of the ♣K is immaterial. So long as the diamond finesse succeeds, West is home. When the ◇Q wins, he cashes the ◇A, ruffs a diamond and throws North in on the third round of trumps, forcing him to lead a club or to concede a ruff and discard.

North: ♠Q1076 ♡QJ9 ◇KJ102 ♣K75
South: ♠AK5 ♡ – ◇9765 ♣96432

65

North doubles 4♠ and leads the ♡2 to South's ♡A. A low heart comes back. West discards the ◇2, not only because a ruff wouldn't help, but because he wants North to be on play. Reluctant to set up a heart in dummy, perhaps, or to open up the clubs, he may switch to a diamond, partner's second suit. A mistake, certainly, but West should give him the chance to make it, for it's his only hope of scoring eight tricks. The other hands could be:

North: ♠752 ♡K62 ◇J63 ♣A642
South: ♠A9 ♡AQ853 ◇K1097 ♣K10

Against the best defence West could be kept to six tricks, but any penalty would be excessive against a contract opponents can't make. Such is often the case, so when you are tempted to sacrifice, make sure first that it isn't a phantom.

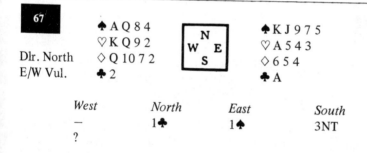

66

Dlr. West
N/S Vul.

♠ A
♡ J 7 6 5 4
♦ A J 9 7
♣ J 7 2

♠ K 8 7 2
♡ A
♦ K Q 10 2
♣ A 6 5 3

West	East
1♡	1♠
2♦	3♣
3NT	4♦
?	

No question of passing. You opened on the flimsiest of values but the sequence is unmistakably forcing. What's more your hand has improved considerably. East must be short in hearts. He may even have a void, the ideal fig leaf to hide your threadbare suit. Head high, bid 5♦.

67

Dlr. North
E/W Vul.

♠ A Q 8 4
♡ K Q 9 2
♦ Q 10 7 2
♣ 2

♠ K J 9 7 5
♡ A 5 4 3
♦ 6 5 4
♣ A

West	North	East	South
–	1♣	1♠	3NT
?			

Of course South is spoofing. Allowing for any sort of opening by North and a minimum vulnerable overcall by East, South can have at best 6 points, probably less. If you double, the obvious move, South will quickly escape into 4♣ and so convey to North a good picture of his hand — a lot of shape and few, if any, high cards. Ignore him. Bid 4♠.

66

North, intent to wound and not afraid to strike, leads a trump. You have eleven tricks — the ♠AK, the ♡A, the ♣A and seven tricks on a cross-ruff, so long as you get the timing right.

Let's get it wrong first. Start with the ♠A, then the ♡A. After ruffing two spades and two hearts you will be in dummy, unable to get back without letting in the enemy, and another trump lead will quickly kill your third heart ruff.

But, of course, you worked it out at trick two and began with the ♡A. Now you could ruff three hearts in dummy, getting back with the ♠A and two spade ruffs.

North: ♠Q106 ♡Q109 ◇543 ♣K1084
South: ♠J9543 ♡K832 ◇86 ♣Q9

What's the secret of correct timing? Like so much else in bridge it is largely a question of looking ahead and going through the motions mentally before embarking on the play.

67

South leads the ◇9 against 4♠ and finds North with ◇AKJ3. A fourth diamond is ruffed high by East who draws trumps, North having three, South a singleton. The contract depends on not losing a heart. How should South tackle the suit?

It's a simple matter of card-reading. North has shown three spades and four diamonds. He bid 1♣, so he should have more clubs than diamonds. That accounts for twelve cards, leaving room for one heart (or none).

North: ♠1032 ♡6 ◇AKJ3 ♣KQ1083
South: ♠6 ♡J1087 ◇98 ♣J97654

East should lay down the ♡A, and if all follow low, finesse the nine, unless South inserts an honour in which case the finesse is repeated.

Observe that if West wastes a round of bidding by doubling 3NT, North, knowing exactly what's going on, may well sacrifice in 5♣ — for one down.

68

Dlr. East
E/W Vul.

♠ J 5 4
♡ Q J 10 9 4
◇ Q J
♣ A Q 2

```
    N
 W     E
    S
```

♠ 8 3 2
♡ A 8 7 6
◇ A 3
♣ K 5 4 3

West	North	East	South
—	—	Pass	Pass
1♡	Pass	3♡	Pass
?			

It's close. West has little to spare, but a good trump fit is always encouraging and an enterprising bidder will surely call the game. If he could see dummy he would regret it, for he will need two finesses or one finesse and a 3-3 break — not an attractive prospect. Against that, the duplication in spades is unlucky. Change dummy's ♠2 into the ◇2 and it would be a pretty good contract.

69

Dlr. North
Both Vul.

♠ A J 7 5
♡ A J 3 2
◇ K 8 4
♣ 9 7

```
    N
 W     E
    S
```

♠ 6 2
♡ Q 9 8 4
◇ A
♣ A K 8 6 4 3

West	North	East	South
—	Pass	1♣	Pass
1♡	Pass	3♡	Pass
3♠	Pass	4◇	Pass
?			

There should be enough for a slam. All the controls are there, but West may be worried about the quality of his trumps. If so, he should bid 5♡. East recognises it as a specific enquiry about trumps, nothing else. His holding should suffice opposite KJxx or A10xx, so he bids the slam.

68

North leads the ♠K, the ♠A and ♠7 to South's ♠Q. A club comes back. Declarer negotiates successfully the trump finesse, finding North with ♡K53, and now it rests with the diamonds. Should West test the clubs, and if they don't break 3-3, take the fateful finesse? It sounds reasonable, but the diamond finesse is unlikely to succeed. North has shown impeccable spades and 10 points already. With another king he might well have doubled 1♡, so, far from being a 50-50 chance, the diamond finesse is an outsider.

There is, however, a promising alternative. Declarer cashes the ♢A, comes to hand with a club and plays off his two remaining trumps, leaving himself with ♢Q ♣2 and dummy with ♣K3. If South started with the ♢K and long clubs, he is squeezed, the victim of a *Vienna Coup* as in (**52**).

69

North leads the ♢Q. At trick two, on the ♡4, South produces the ♡K. Unless he is a very wily player, it's a singleton. How should declarer proceed?

If clubs break 3-2 there's no problem, but some of the time (28 per cent) they'll split 4-1. West should visualise this unfriendly distribution.

> North: ♠K1093 ♡10765 ♢QJ109 ♣J
> South: ♠Q84 ♡K ♢76532 ♣Q1052

Allowing for it, he leads a club to dummy's ace and a *low* club. South's return is immaterial. Say it's a spade, West wins, throws dummy's second spade on the ♢K and takes the marked finesse in hearts. Next he ruffs a club with the ♡J and uses his last trump to finesse again. The ♡Q removes North's last trump and all the clubs are winners.

70

♠ Q 10 8 7 5 4
♡ K 3 2
◇ A 6 5 3
♣ —

Dlr. East
Both Vul.

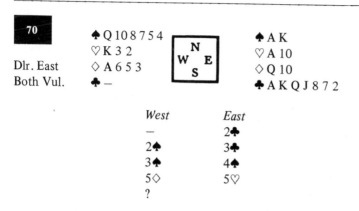

♠ A K
♡ A 10
◇ Q 10
♣ A K Q J 8 7 2

West	East
—	2♣
2♠	3♣
3♠	4♠
5◇	5♡
?	

All West wants to know is whether or not East has the ♠AK, so he puts the question with 5NT, the Grand Slam Force, and East duly bids 7♠.

71

♠ 6 3
♡ Q 8 7 4
◇ A K Q 5 4 3
♣ J

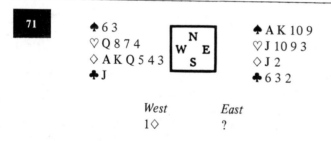

♠ A K 10 9
♡ J 10 9 3
◇ J 2
♣ 6 3 2

West	East
1◇	?

Bid 1♡. If you bid 1♠ the heart fit may be lost. A spade fit wouldn't be. Reverse West's majors and over 1♡ he would bid 1♠.

70

The ♣10 is led. What can go wrong? Only a bad trump break. If North has ♠Jxxx there's no remedy, but if the danger comes from South it can be parried. West will need three entries in dummy, two to reduce his trumps and one more to go over for the kill. There is, however, a complication. West must dispose of four losers and if South ruffs a club, after dummy's last entry has gone, West will catch the ♠J, but he will have losers instead in the red suits.

The lucky club lead takes the place of an extra entry. West ruffs, crosses to the ♠A and ruffs another club. Looking ahead, he cashes the ◇A and ♡K before going over to the ♠K. If North shows out, as feared, West reels off five clubs — throwing first three diamonds, then a heart. If South doesn't ruff the last club West throws his last heart and the ♡A or the ◇Q applies the *coup de grâce*.

> North: ♠2 ♡QJ764 ◇KJ ♣109654
> South: ♠J963 ♡985 ◇98742 ♣3

71

A 4-4 fit is a source of strength against which the best defence is often powerless. Here East-West are unlikely to bid game, yet with hearts as trumps ten tricks will usually be made.

If defenders attack trumps, declarer will score ten top tricks. Should they lead clubs to punch dummy — the West hand — declarer will cross in spades and ruff the last club himself before leading trumps. He will still retain a trump to deal with a fourth club, if need be.

It is because the 4-4 trump fit puts declarer in so strong a position that every effort is made to bring it to light in the bidding. Hence Stayman and Baron.

Like other good things, however, the quest for 4-4 fits can be carried too far and players are apt to disdain 4-3 fits, which are often preferable to no-trumps. True, they require more skill in play, but that's another matter.

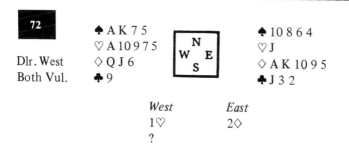

72

Dlr. West
Both Vul.

♠ A K 7 5
♡ A 10 9 7 5
◇ Q J 6
♣ 9

♠ 10 8 6 4
♡ J
◇ A K 10 9 5
♣ J 3 2

West	East
1♡	2◇
?	

Forget about points. Bid 2♠. Yes, it is in every sense a *reverse*, a term surrounded by much mumbo-jumbo.

A sequence, in an uncontested auction, in which a new suit, higher in rank than the first, is bid at the two level shows strength because partner may have to give preference at the level of three on a minimum. Usually a reverse by opener promises 16-17 points. But it's a promise *by inference*, not a convention, still less a mystique. Here you have only 14 points but the diamond fit is worth several more. And, knowing your shape, partner will be reluctant to support you without four trumps.

73

Dlr. West
Love All

♠ Q 5 3
♡ J 10 5
◇ A K Q J
♣ K 7 5

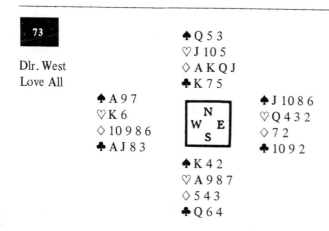

♠ A 9 7
♡ K 6
◇ 10 9 8 6
♣ A J 8 3

♠ J 10 8 6
♡ Q 4 3 2
◇ 7 2
♣ 10 9 2

♠ K 4 2
♡ A 9 8 7
◇ 5 4 3
♣ Q 6 4

West bids 1NT (12/14) and North doubles. To wriggle out of the impending disaster East bids 2◇, and when that is doubled he *redoubles* — an SOS calling on West to rescue.

72

East, with a healthy respect for reverses, bids 4♠. North leads the ♣K, then the ♣A. Declarer ruffs and lays down the ♠AK. The second time, North throws a club.

Having reversed boldly on 14 points and reached game on the slenderest values, West has the misfortune to run into a 4-1 trump break. What are his prospects?

On the face of it, he should be in trouble, yet such is the power of well-fitting hands that he cannot be beaten.

North: ♠2 ♡K843 ◇732 ♣AK875
South: ♠QJ93 ♡Q62 ◇84 ♣Q1064

Crossing in diamonds, West ruffs dummy's third club with his last trump and plays on diamonds. South can ruff and force dummy but, persisting with diamonds, West will always be a move ahead.

The play justifies the bidding and the importance attached by West to his fit. Exchange his holding in the minors and a modest 2♡ would have been his rebid.

73

In 1NT doubled, West cannot expect to make more than four tricks. In response to East's SOS West bids 2♠, for East is prepared for a major, and by so doing he avoids the three level. South may bid 3NT, an easy contract, but he may well double. He surely would if opponents were vulnerable. What would happen?

North would start with the ◇K and switch to the ♡J. Winning, West would play back a diamond and North would continue hearts. Declarer would ruff the third heart, ruff a diamond and run the ♣10 to North's ♣K. A diamond return would ensure two trump tricks for the defence, one down — very different from three down in 1NT! A slip in defence and the contract might even be made.

Playing a weak no-trump, which many top-ranking players do regardless of vulnerability, the SOS redouble is an invaluable weapon.

74

♠ 1096432
♡ —
♢ Q 4 3
♣ A 9 7 6

Dlr. West
Both Vul.

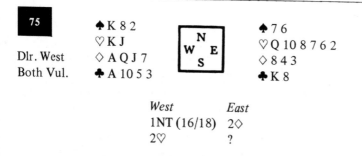

♠ 7 5
♡ A K 6
♢ K 7 5 2
♣ K Q 10 3

West	North	East	South
Pass	Pass	1NT (15/17)	Pass
?			

A weakness take-out into 2♠, which partner must pass, will absolve you of all blame at the inquest. And yet, if partner has the right cards, you could make 4♠. There's no way of finding out, for he couldn't pass 3♠ and you would rightly take him out of 3NT. Whatever he did you would end up in 4♠. If you saw his hand you wouldn't be so ambitious, but you can't, so — take a chance! A comforting thought is that come what may, you are unlikely to be doubled.

75

♠ K 8 2
♡ K J
♢ A Q J 7
♣ A 10 5 3

Dlr. West
Both Vul.

♠ 7 6
♡ Q 10 8 7 6 2
♢ 8 4 3
♣ K 8

West	East
1NT (16/18)	2♢
2♡	?

Using transfers (see **13**), Oswald Jacoby, father of the convention, was playing this hand many years ago with his son Jim, world champion to be.

Not good enough for 4♡ over 1NT, yet with something to spare for a mere weakness take-out, Ozzie bid 2♢. The transfer enabled him, in effect, to bid ♡2½. With a maximum and a fit Jim called 3♡, converted by Ozzie to 4♡.

74

The sight of dummy, with the ♡AK facing your void, is thoroughly depressing. The lead of the ◇J largely makes up for it. You play low from dummy, expecting South to have the ◇A and to duck. He does, rightly so from his angle. Heaving a sigh of relief, you win, cross in clubs and park two diamonds on the ♡AK. A 3-2 trump break now sees you home.

North: ♠AQ8 ♡J9542 ◇J109 ♣J2
South: ♠KJ ♡Q10873 ◇A86 ♣854

The lesson to be drawn is that there's an imponderable factor working for declarer. Defending in the dark, the best opponents are apt to give something away, especially on the opening lead. This advantage shrinks rapidly when scientific bidding pinpoints every card, but it can be decisive when, as above, a direct sequence gives nothing away.

So when in doubt, don't hesitate — weigh the imponderable.

75

North led the ♡A and ♡9. Unblocking on the ace, Jim Jacoby drew the remaining trump from dummy, discarding a spade, and continued with the ♣K, ♣A and a club ruff, just in case a defender had ♣QJx. No such luck. The diamond finesse failed and the ♣J came back.

Things didn't look promising. West's defensive lead and play, and South's low-key discards, all pointed to the ♠A being over the ♠K. Jim played accordingly. After ruffing the ♣J, he cashed dummy's last trump, baring his ♠K.

North: ♠A104 ♡A9 ◇K962 ♣J742
South: ♠QJ953 ♡543 ◇105 ♣Q96

To keep two diamonds, North bared his ♠A. Now came the ◇A, picking up South's ◇10, and the ♠K, throwing in North, who had to lead from ◇96 into Jim Jacoby's tenace. Well bid and well played.

76

You are still playing transfers.

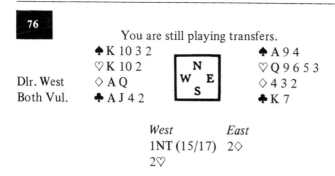

```
                ♠ K 10 3 2              ♠ A 9 4
                ♡ K 10 2               ♡ Q 9 6 5 3
Dlr. West       ◇ A Q         N        ◇ 4 3 2
Both Vul.       ♣ A J 4 2  W     E     ♣ K 7
                              S
```

West	East
1NT (15/17)	2◇
2♡	

East should bid 2NT. West will then know that, in addition to five hearts, he has a balanced hand, suitable for no-trumps. With a minimum, West passes or bids 3♡. With more, he chooses between 4♡ and 3NT. The lead will run up to him anyway, but let's say he bids 3NT.

77

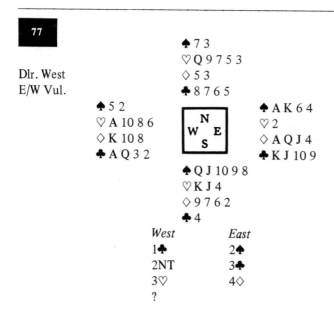

```
                            ♠ 7 3
                            ♡ Q 9 7 5 3
Dlr. West                   ◇ 5 3
E/W Vul.                    ♣ 8 7 6 5
            ♠ 5 2                          ♠ A K 6 4
            ♡ A 10 8 6         N           ♡ 2
            ◇ K 10 8     W           E     ◇ A Q J 4
            ♣ A Q 3 2         S           ♣ K J 10 9
                            ♠ Q J 10 9 8
                            ♡ K J 4
                            ◇ 9 7 6 2
                            ♣ 4
```

West	East
1♣	2♠
2NT	3♣
3♡	4◇
?	

Having shown a minimum with 2NT, West's 3♡ promises nothing extra so East's 4◇ is a slamward move. With no reason to hold back, West should bid 5◇. East now applies the Grand Slam Force, 5NT, leading to 7♣.

76

North leads the ♣9. He is unlikely to have the ♣Q, but declarer should resist the temptation to make sure. He needs to develop at least three tricks in hearts before South can attack his ♢AQ, his Achilles' heel. That means playing hearts from dummy, finessing the ♡10, at trick two. If North has the ♡J he can do no harm. His best return is another heart, but should South have the ♡A, a diamond switch would no longer be dangerous. If North has the ♢K the club finesse, pretty well certain to succeed, will still bring the contract home.

In 4♡, with the opening lead from South, East as declarer would have greater problems. Here the transfer is a help, but it isn't always so. There's a price to pay. The artificial bid allows opponents to double, without risk, to call for a lead or sometimes to pave the way for a sacrifice.

77

When this hand came up in a match, North led a trump — won in dummy. With eleven top tricks, West looked to a dummy reversal for two more. So he cashed the ♠AK, ruffed a spade high, crossed in trumps and ruffed another spade high. All that remained was to go to dummy, draw trumps and claim. Alas . . .

Can you see what happened? North discarded his two diamonds on the spades and when declarer tried to get to dummy with a diamond, the only entry, North ruffed. Bad luck? No, lack of forethought, often the same thing. West would have to use diamonds as an entry some time, so he should have done it the first time, while North still had a diamond.

78

	♠ A 7 4		♠ 5 3 2
	♡ K Q J 10 8		♡ 9 7 6 5
Dlr. North	♢ K 4 2		♢ A J 9
E/W Vul.	♣ A 6		♣ K 8 4

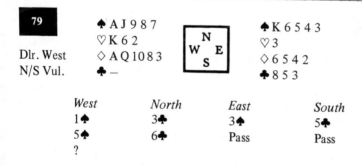

West	North	East	South
—	Pass	Pass	Pass
1♡	1♠	2♡	Pass
?			

West is worth just 4♡ but he should make allowances for East, who may have had a problem in finding a bid over 1♠. His raise may be shaded. A trial bid is the better action. Here 3♢ would suggest game if East had anything useful in that suit. East jumps unhesitatingly to 4♡. Had West bid 2NT, or 2♠ for that matter, East wouldn't have been quite so happy.

79

	♠ A J 9 8 7		♠ K 6 5 4 3
	♡ K 6 2		♡ 3
Dlr. West	♢ A Q 10 8 3		♢ 6 5 4 2
N/S Vul.	♣ —		♣ 8 5 3

West	North	East	South
1♠	3♣	3♠	5♣
5♠	6♣	Pass	Pass
?			

It doesn't look as if North-South can make twelve tricks, but on freak hands, and especially at this vulnerability, the insurance premium is well worthwhile. In the slam zone, when in doubt, buy the contract. It pays in the long run, so bid 6♠. North doubles.

78

North leads the ♠K. West wins and plays the ♡K. North goes up with the ♡A, cashes the ♠QJ, South throwing a club the second time, and exits with another heart, South following.

With three tricks stacked against him, West can't afford to lose a diamond. Should he, therefore, finesse? There seems to be no alternative. On reflection, however, declarer will realise that North can't have the ◇Q. He has shown up already with ♠KQJ106 and ♡A, a maximum pass. With another queen he would have surely opened 1♠.

But though North can't have the ◇Q he could have the ◇10 and that might be enough. West crosses to the ♣K and leads the ◇J, intending to run it, unless South covers. He does, so West wins and finesses against the ◇10, hoping to find this distribution:

> North: ♠KQJ106 ♡A4 ◇1073 ♣952
> South: ♠98 ♡32 ◇Q865 ♣QJ1073

79

North leads the ♣2. West ruffs and . . . ?

If trumps are 3-0 West must start with the ♠K, for only if South is the culprit can the queen be caught. But the situation is transformed by the lead of the ♣2, an unmistakable suit preference signal. North is underleading his honours to put South in for the return of a diamond, which he will ruff. So he must have a trump, and starting with the ♠K would serve no purpose. But there's an even better reason for playing the ♠A first. West needs three certain entries in dummy for finesses in diamonds. The ♠K is one. Heart ruffs will provide two more.

> North: ♠Q10 ♡A10754 ◇ – ♣KQJ1072
> South: ♠2 ♡QJ8 ◇KJ97 ♣A964

West will finesse the ◇8 the first time, then the ◇10 and finally the ◇Q. Declarer should always be on the *qui vive* to intercept defenders' signals and profit by them.

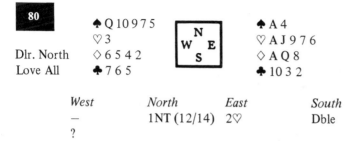

	80			
	♠ Q 10 9 7 5		♠ A 4	
	♡ 3		♡ A J 9 7 6	
Dlr. North	◇ 6 5 4 2		◇ A Q 8	
Love All	♣ 7 6 5		♣ 10 3 2	

West	North	East	South
—	1NT (12/14)	2♡	Dble
?			

I hope you don't belong to the 'I never rescue' brigade. With ♠AKxx(x) you pass serenely, for you bring partner two tricks. Here you bring none and the combined hands will surely produce at least two tricks more in spades than in hearts. That is the time to rescue.

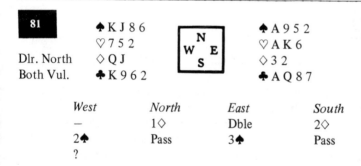

	81			
	♠ K J 8 6		♠ A 9 5 2	
	♡ 7 5 2		♡ A K 6	
Dlr. North	◇ Q J		◇ 3 2	
Both Vul.	♣ K 9 6 2		♣ A Q 8 7	

West	North	East	South
—	1◇	Dble	2◇
2♠	Pass	3♠	Pass
?			

Have you not 10 points, enough to bid game and hold your head high if you go down? The answer is: No. Your 10 points are a mirage. The ◇QJ are worthless and so is the fact that it's a doubleton, for your partner must be short, too. Your effective count is 7 and your distribution is flat. Pass.

Beware of doubleton queens and knaves. When they are in a suit bid by opponents discount them altogether.

80

Against 2♠ North leads the ♣K, the ♣A and ♣9. South, having signalled with the ♣Q, wins with the ♣J and leads the ♡K.

West looks through the backs of the cards. Since South has shown up with ♣QJx, ♡K, and ♡Q, by inference, North must have the two other kings for his 1NT. West can probably get out for one down, but if South has the ♠J — more likely than not — he can actually make the contract!

Winning the fourth trick with the ♡A, he ruffs a heart, finesses the ◇Q and ruffs another. Next comes the ♠Q, covered by North and won with dummy's ♠A. A third heart ruff follows, leaving West with the ♠10 bare. Crossing to the ◇A he leads dummy's last heart and scores the ♠10 *en passant*.

North: ♠K6 ♡542 ◇K973 ♣AK98
South: ♠J832 ♡KQ108 ◇J10 ♣QJ4

81

North leads the ◇AK and switches to the ♡Q. Since you are in 3♠, you can afford to lose one trump trick, but not two, so you make a routine safety play — the ♠K — then low to dummy's ♠9. If it loses to South's ♠10, the ♠Q will fall the next time.

Suppose that South shows out. Your remaining problem is to bring in the clubs without loss and, as with the trumps, the danger is a 4-1 split. North is known to have the nine, and probably ten cards that are not clubs — four or more diamonds, four spades and a heart — so he is likely to be short in clubs and may well have a singleton. Start with the ♣A, then the ♣Q, to allow for this distribution.

North: ♠Q1074 ♡QJ10 ◇AK654 ♣10
South: ♠3 ♡9843 ◇10987 ♣J543

82

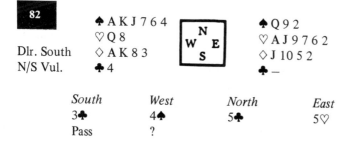

Dlr. South
N/S Vul.

♠ A K J 7 6 4
♡ Q 8
◇ A K 8 3
♣ 4

♠ Q 9 2
♡ A J 9 7 6 2
◇ J 10 5 2
♣ —

South	West	North	East
3♣	4♠	5♣	5♡
Pass	?		

Time was when East's 5♡ would have promised a long, powerful suit, without implying spade support. Today it is essentially a cue-bid, agreeing spades and inviting a slam. This is only logical. It cannot be rewarding to compete with partner at the five level, and the chance to make a constructive cue-bid shouldn't be missed. Bid 6♠.

83

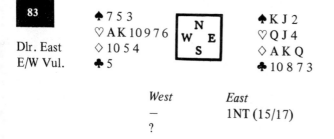

Dlr. East
E/W Vul.

♠ 7 5 3
♡ A K 10 9 7 6
◇ 10 5 4
♣ 5

♠ K J 2
♡ Q J 4
◇ A K Q
♣ 10 8 7 3

West	East
—	1NT (15/17)
?	

If the hearts were a minor, West would bid 3NT. Even with a major there's much to be said for the same response as it's easier to make nine tricks than ten and there's nothing to spare here in high cards. Having the lead run up to East is another consideration. Against that is the singleton club. In a suit contract it's a control. In no-trumps it's a serious liability and can be fatal. It's fairly close, but let's bid 4♡.

82

North led a club, ruffed in dummy. West drew trumps, finding South with three, and ran the ♡Q, losing to South who returned a club. West ruffed, cashed another trump and crossed to the hearts. He had left: ♠6 ◇AK83. When South showed out in hearts, West fell back on the diamond finesse. One down.

> North: ♠3 ♡ 10543 ◇Q97 ♣K9752
> South: ♠1085 ♡K ◇64 ♣AQJ10863

Declarer, when this hand came up, was a distinguished American international. Can you see where he went wrong?

South, who was surely marked with seven clubs for his vulnerable 3♣ bid, had shown three spades and one heart, eleven cards that were not diamonds. So unless the ◇Q dropped, the finesse couldn't succeed. But if the hearts were 4-1 — and if they broke 3-2, nothing mattered — North would be inexorably squeezed in the red suits, providing that West played his last spade before his second heart. What happened was that he 'forgot' to play the squeeze card!

83

North leads the ♣K, then the ♣Q. West ruffs and draws trumps in two rounds. What distribution, if any, could endanger the contract?

None. Neither will West be put to any guess. Having drawn trumps he crosses to the ◇A and ruffs a club. Next he cashes the ◇KQ and ruffs dummy's last club. This leaves him with: ♠753 ♡K facing ♠KJ2 ♡Q in dummy.

He leads a spade and inserts whichever honour is nearest his thumb. It's immaterial. South wins but must now return a spade to dummy's other honour or concede a ruff and discard.

This is a classical end-play. First the side-suits are eliminated so that the victim has no safe exit. Then he is thrown in.

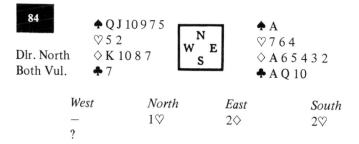

84

♠ Q J 10 9 7 5
♡ 5 2
Dlr. North   ◇ K 10 8 7
Both Vul.   ♣ 7

♠ A
♡ 7 6 4
◇ A 6 5 4 3 2
♣ A Q 10

West	North	East	South
–	1♡	2◇	2♡
?			

Opponents have found a fit in hearts and may find another in clubs, so sooner or later you will have to compete at the four level, if not higher. Go all the way at once. Bid 4♠, restricting the enemy's room for manoeuvre. In spades you can outbid them at the same level, so there's no need to reveal the fit in diamonds.

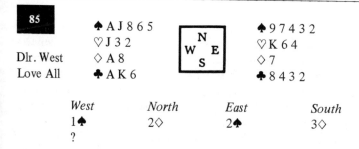

85

♠ A J 8 6 5
♡ J 3 2
Dlr. West   ◇ A 8
Love All   ♣ A K 6

♠ 9 7 4 3 2
♡ K 6 4
◇ 7
♣ 8 4 3 2

West	North	East	South
1♠	2◇	2♠	3◇
?			

Are you worth 4♠? Not quite, for partner's raise may be shaded. And yet, if you bid 3♠ you will be merely competing and partner will pass even with something to spare. How can you find out whether his raise was minimal or full-blooded? Bid 3♡. Spades having been agreed, another suit – it has to be hearts at the three level – is only introduced as an invitation. East signs off in 3♠.

84

North leads the ♡K, and switches to the ◇J. South having signalled with the ♡Q, the writing is on the wall. North will come in with the ♠K, put South in with a heart and ruff a diamond. What's to be done?

The club finesse immediately suggests itself, allowing West to discard his second heart, so cutting enemy communications. True, but if North has the ♣K, the finesse is unnecessary. West can cash the ♣A, throw his heart on the ♣Q and achieve the same result. This way, however, he doubles his chances, for if South turns up with the ♣K, instead of going two down, West can ruff, cross to the ♠A and lead the ♣10. Unless South has both the ♣K and ♣J, West discards his heart, a loser on a loser, and is safe. If South has the ♠K there's no prophylactic, but the distribution could be:

North: ♠K432 ♡AK983 ◇J ♣J98
South: ♠86 ♡QJ10 ◇Q9 ♣K65432

85

North leads the ◇K. West wins and lays down the ♠A, both defenders following. He has a trump to lose, a club and three possible losers in hearts if he has to tackle the suit himself. There's no certain way of making the contract, but declarer can get very near it by *partial elimination*. He ruffs his second diamond, cashes the ♠AK and exits with a trump. Unless the defender with the winning trump started with four or more clubs, all is well, for he must either concede a ruff and discard or open up the hearts.

North: ♠KQ ♡Q105 ◇KQJ432 ♣Q9
South: ♠10 ♡A987 ◇10965 ♣J1075

If clubs are 3-3, defenders can cash a club but are then in the same position as before. Meanwhile, a club winner has been set up in dummy.

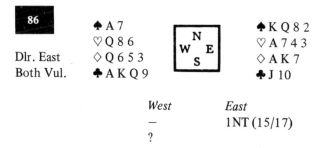

86	♠ A 7		♠ K Q 8 2
	♡ Q 8 6	N	♡ A 7 4 3
Dlr. East	◇ Q 6 5 3	W E	◇ A K 7
Both Vul.	♣ A K Q 9	S	♣ J 10

West	East
—	1 NT (15/17)
?	

Unless East has something over a minimum a slam is unlikely, so West bids 4NT — always quantitative when no suit has been agreed — inviting partner to go on if he has anything to spare. With a maximum, as here, East bids 6NT. There's no 4-4 fit anywhere, so neither Stayman nor Baron (see **16**) would have led to a better contract.

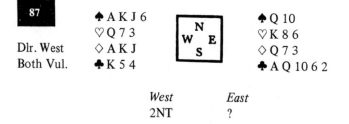

87	♠ A K J 6		♠ Q 10
	♡ Q 7 3	N	♡ K 8 6
Dlr. West	◇ A K J	W E	◇ Q 7 3
Both Vul.	♣ K 5 4	S	♣ A Q 10 6 2

West	East
2NT	?

Bid a direct 6NT. There should be enough material to generate twelve tricks. Suppose that you were even stronger, with the ♡A instead of the ♡K and perhaps the ♣J as well. How would you invite a grand slam? The answer is to bid 5NT. The inference is unmistakable. If you were looking for a small slam you would bid 4NT, so 5NT can only be an invitation to a grand slam. If opener doesn't like it, he signs off in 6NT!

86.

South leads the ♡J. Before that lead it looked as if the slam would depend on one of two chances — the ♡K on the right side or a 3-3 diamond break. Now the first and best hope has gone, for clearly South didn't start with the ♡KJ. The odds against a 3-3 diamond break are 2-1. Can East improve on them?

Yes — so long as he allows the ♡J to hold. The ♡10, no doubt, will follow — not that it matters a great deal. Low from dummy, the ♡A from East, who tests the diamonds, finding South with four.

The contract is unbeatable! After two hearts, three diamonds and four clubs, dummy remains with ♠A7 ♡Q ◇6 and declarer with ♠KQ82. North must retain the ♡K, South the ◇J. Neither defender can keep four spades, so the ♠2 brings in the twelfth trick, and all because declarer *rectified the count* at trick one.

87

North leads the ◇10 against 6NT. Winning in hand, West plays the ♣4 to dummy's ♣A and the ♣2 back to his ♣K. North throws a diamond. Unlucky. Without a fourth trick in clubs declarer will be one short and he can't afford to give up a club, for opponents would then promptly cash the ♡A.

Do prospects look bleak? They needn't do, for declarer still has an even-money chance — finding South with the ♡A. After the ♣K, he crosses to the ♠Q and leads a low heart. If South rises with the ♡A, West has twelve tricks. So he plays low. Now West proceeds to cash his winners in spades and diamonds. Ten cards have gone. In the 3-card ending South remains with the ♡A ♣J9. A heart throws him in, forcing him to lead into dummy's ♣Q10.

North: ♠98543 ♡952 ◇10982 ♣7
South: ♠72 ♡AJ104 ◇654 ♣J983

88

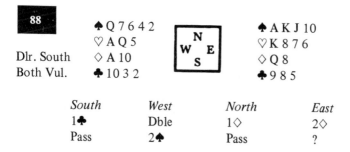

♠ Q 7 6 4 2
♡ A Q 5
◇ A 10
♣ 10 3 2

Dlr. South
Both Vul.

♠ A K J 10
♡ K 8 7 6
◇ Q 8
♣ 9 8 5

South	West	North	East
1♣	Dble	1◇	2◇
Pass	2♠	Pass	?

East's 2◇ cue-bid promises no more than 10 points or so and invites West to pick the major, but it's not forcing to game and with a minimum, as here, West would pass a raise to 3♠. East should, therefore, jump to 4♠.

89

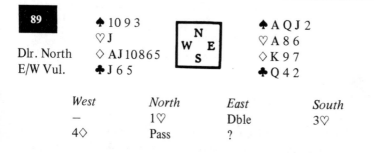

♠ 10 9 3
♡ J
◇ A J 10 8 6 5
♣ J 6 5

Dlr. North
E/W Vul.

♠ A Q J 2
♡ A 8 6
◇ K 9 7
♣ Q 4 2

West	North	East	South
—	1♡	Dble	3♡
4◇	Pass	?	

East has little to spare for his take-out double and too much can't be expected of West, who had to speak at the four level. Against that, the spade finesse is probably right and a heart loser is unlikely. It's a close decision, but aggression usually pays, so let's bid 5◇.

88

North leads the ♣Q. South overtakes, cashes the ♣K and ♣J, North discarding two diamonds, and switches to the ♡J. West draws trumps, finding South with three. At first sight, the contract hinges on a 3-3 heart break, but that's impossible. South has shown nine black cards, and three hearts would leave him with one diamond. North simply cannot have eight!

South needs the ◇K for his opening, however, though not necessarily the ◇J, and that presents declarer with another option.

> North: ♠8 ♡109432 ◇J76543 ♣Q
> South: ♠953 ♡J ◇K92 ♣AKJ764

West leads dummy's ◇Q, which South must cover. West wins and cashes his two trumps. His last three cards are ♡Q5 ◇10 facing ♡K87 in dummy. Unless North has parted with the ◇J he can only have two hearts.

This was a *transfer squeeze*, the diamond menace being transferred from dummy to declarer.

Were West to place North with the ◇K he would cash the ◇A, leaving the ◇Q in dummy, and North, discarding first, would be the victim of a simple positional squeeze.

89

North leads the ♡3 and that one card should tell West all he needs to know. From a suit headed by the KQ North wouldn't have led a low one. So South is marked with one of the tops. With ♣AK North would have doubtless led a club, if only to look at dummy before committing himself. It follows that South has the ♣K or ♣A. To have scratched up the lightest opening North needs the ◇Q. Alternatively, if he is very distributional, say 3-5-0-5, he has a void. West should cater for both possibilities by coming to hand with a heart ruff and leading the ◇J. If North follows, he runs it.

> North: ♠K ♡K9532 ◇Q432 ♣A103
> South: ♠87654 ♡Q1074 ◇ — ♣K987

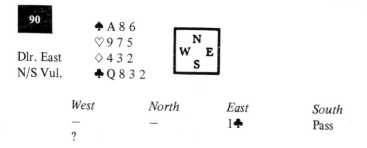

90	♠ A 8 6			
	♡ 9 7 5			
Dlr. East	◊ 4 3 2			
N/S Vul.	♣ Q 8 3 2			

West	North	East	South
—	—	1♣	Pass
?			

You are just too good to pass, yet seemingly not good enough to do anything else. A 1NT response suggests four clubs, but also 8-10 points. This isn't a convention but simple logic, because it is an *expensive* bid. Even 1♠ is better, but the cheapest bid, 1◊, is the best. If East is weak, the final contract will be 1NT or 2♣, unless, of course, North-South step in. What if, excited by a glorious fit, East soars to 5◊? Frightening?

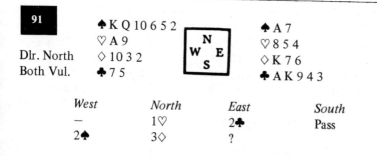

91	♠ K Q 10 6 5 2		♠ A 7
	♡ A 9		♡ 8 5 4
Dlr. North	◊ 10 3 2		◊ K 7 6
Both Vul.	♣ 7 5		♣ A K 9 4 3

West	North	East	South
—	1♡	2♣	Pass
2♠	3◊	?	

Opponents seem unlikely to make nine tricks, but a speculative double for one down is greedy. The choice lies between passing and competing with 3♠. The latter has the edge, for partner, who hasn't passed, may be good enough to call the game. Over 3♠ West duly does so.

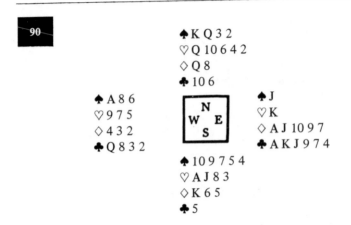

90

♠ K Q 3 2
♡ Q 10 6 4 2
◇ Q 8
♣ 10 6

♠ A 8 6
♡ 9 7 5
◇ 4 3 2
♣ Q 8 3 2

N
W E
S

♠ J
♡ K
◇ A J 10 9 7
♣ A K J 9 7 4

♠ 10 9 7 5 4
♡ A J 8 3
◇ K 6 5
♣ 5

So long as the diamonds break 3-2 and the honours are split, or North has both, 5◇ can't be beaten.

91

North leads the ♡K against 4♠. West assumes the ◇A to be on the right side, but that still leaves him with a heart and two diamonds to lose, so he must bring in the trumps without loss. North has advertised ten, maybe eleven, red cards. But has he one club and two spades or vice-versa? How can West find out?

The ♡K is allowed to hold. Winning the heart continuation, declarer leads a club to the ♣A. Back with a heart ruff, he plays a second club. Should North ruff, a losing diamond will be parked on the ♣K. If he follows, West will finesse against the ♠J.

North: ♠9 ♡KQJ76 ◇AQ854 ♣102
South: ♠J843 ♡1032 ◇J9 ♣QJ86

What if on the second club North throws a red card? Now West must guess, but he should play North for two spades. With a singleton the temptation to ruff might have proved too great.

92

Dlr. North
E/W Vul.

♠ A J 3
♡ Q 10 8 2
◇ A Q J
♣ A 10 3

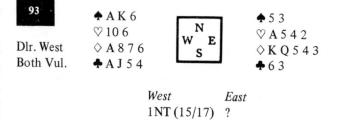

♠ 7 6 4
♡ K 3
◇ 9 5
♣ Q J 9 8 5 4

West	North	East	South
—	Pass	Pass	1♡
Dble	Pass	2♣	Pass
?			

East has promised nothing, so there's a case for passing, but, sitting over the opening bid, West's honours are well placed and he might venture 2NT. Expecting something close to an opening 2NT, East raises to 3NT. If the clubs work, it should be easy. If they don't, even 2NT could be at risk.

93

Dlr. West
Both Vul.

♠ A K 6
♡ 10 6
◇ A 8 7 6
♣ A J 5 4

♠ 5 3
♡ A 5 4 2
◇ K Q 5 4 3
♣ 6 3

West	East
1NT (15/17)	?

The ◇KQ combination heading a 5-card suit is worth more than its face value. Against that, the hand is woefully anaemic in intermediaries, so precious in no-trumps. Bid 2NT. Let West decide.

Observe that playing a weak no-trump, West opens 1◇ and rebids 1NT over 1♡. Now East's diamond holding justifies a raise to game. Since West cannot have a 4-card major — he would have bid 1♠ over 1♡ — he is more likely to have some fit in diamonds.

113

92

North leads the ♡7, low from dummy, and the ♡J from South. West wins. What next? On a lucky day someone would have the doubleton ♣K. On any other it would be held up. The resourceful declarer leads the ♣10, overtaking with the ♣J. It holds, he leads the ♣Q, finessing. South holds up, of course. Still in dummy, West takes the diamond finesse, cashes the ♣A and exits with a heart.

North: ♠Q852 ♡754 ◇76432 ♣2
South: ♠K109 ♡AJ96 ◇K108 ♣K76

South wins with the ♡A and gets off play with the ♠10 to the ♠J and North's ♠Q. West holds off the spade return, wins a third spade, and with a pretty good count of South's hand, cashes the ◇A. If North-South were playing 5-card majors, the ◇K would now drop. They aren't and it doesn't, so West throws South in with it, forcing a lead from ♡96 into his ♡108.

93

West is in 3NT. North leads the ♡K, then the ♡Q, South following. No purpose would be served by ducking again, so West goes up with dummy's ace and turns to the diamonds. He needs all five for his quota and so long as they don't split 4-0, all is well — or is it?

Going through the motions, West sees no problem if the suit breaks 2-2, but what if it's 3-1? Now the suit will be blocked, for apart from the tops, dummy's highest diamond is lower than the lowest in the closed hand. So West lays down the ◇A and crosses to the ◇K. If either defender shows out he leads a heart and jettisons a cumbersome diamond. North cannot have more than three other hearts to cash and meanwhile the diamonds have been unblocked.

North: ♠J94 ♡KQJ97 ◇2 ♣Q1097
South: ♠Q10872 ♡83 ◇J109 ♣K82

94

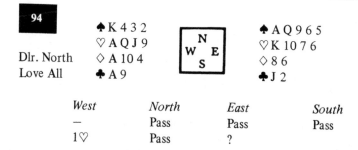

Dlr. North
Love All

♠ K 4 3 2
♡ A Q J 9
◇ A 10 4
♣ A 9

♠ A Q 9 6 5
♡ K 10 7 6
◇ 8 6
♣ J 2

West	North	East	South
—	Pass	Pass	Pass
1♡	Pass	?	

With 4-card support for one major no purpose is served by introducing the other — unless responder has more than enough for a raise to game. Here East is worth 3♡ plus, but he does better to bid 2♠, showing a maximum pass and agreeing hearts by inference. West is worth more than his points suggest, so the final contract will be 6♡.

95

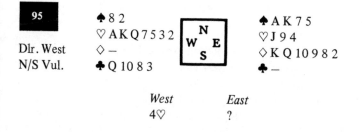

Dlr. West
N/S Vul.

♠ 8 2
♡ A K Q 7 5 3 2
◇ —
♣ Q 10 8 3

♠ A K 7 5
♡ J 9 4
◇ K Q 10 9 8 2
♣ —

West	East
4♡	?

East wants to be in a slam providing that there's no hole in West's hearts. A pre-empt doesn't promise the ace or king. To find out, East makes a cue-bid — 4♠. With such good hearts West can guess that East must be worried about the trumps, so he bids 6♡. Were he to make a cue-bid of 5◇, East would bid the slam — in hearts, needless to say.

115

94

East-West have more spades than hearts between them, but the 4-4 fit is nearly always worth an extra trick. In spades only eleven tricks are available. With hearts as trumps, declarer discards a club on dummy's long spade and ruffs a club — his twelfth trick.

It's easy, and yet a moment's carelessness can cost the contract. The spades could be 4-0. If South has the length, he'll win, but North can be disarmed — so long as West starts with the ♠K. Should South show out, a spade towards dummy will force North to split his honours. Back with the ◇A, West will have a straightforward finesse against North's ♠J(10).

95

North leads the ◇6, the ◇K from dummy, the ◇3 from South. Strange. North wouldn't underlead the ◇A and if South has it, why didn't he play it? The only rational explanation is that, having six diamonds himself, he knew that it would be ruffed.

Can West ruff clubs in dummy? Alas, he would have an insoluble communications problem. To get back at trick two, he would have to ruff a diamond high or North would over-ruff, and he would have to ruff high again after the first club ruff. He cannot afford it.

> North: ♠Q103 ♡1086 ◇6 ♣KJ9765
> South: ♠J964 ♡— ◇AJ7543 ♣A42

Having read the cards, West draws trumps, ending in dummy, and runs the ◇Q unless South covers. He does. West ruffs, crosses to the ♠K and plays the ◇10, setting up two diamonds for club discards with the ♠A as the entry. A club will be his only loser.

96

♠ A J 8 3
♡ K J 10 9 7
◇ 4
♣ 9 5 2

Dlr. West
Both Vul.

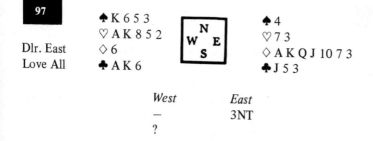

♠ K Q 10 9 6 2
♡ 8
◇ J 8 7
♣ A J 3

West	North	East	South
Pass	Pass	1♠	2♡
?			

You may wonder whether you are worth 3♠ or 4♠, but don't even think of doubling. If you do, North, who must be short in both majors, will bid one of the minors — and find a fit. Given the space, opponents may well outbid you. Don't give them the chance. Bid 4♠. Better one too many than one too few.

97

♠ K 6 5 3
♡ A K 8 5 2
◇ 6
♣ A K 6

Dlr. East
Love All

♠ 4
♡ 7 3
◇ A K Q J 10 7 3
♣ J 5 3

West	East
—	3NT
?	

Fifty years ago an opening 3NT proclaimed a balanced rock-crusher with 25 points or so. Today all but backwoodsmen open 2♣ and rebid 3NT. An opening 3NT shows a solid 7-card minor and little else, as above. West doesn't need any more, so long as the lead doesn't come from South. So, to protect his ♠K, he calls 6◇ and becomes declarer.

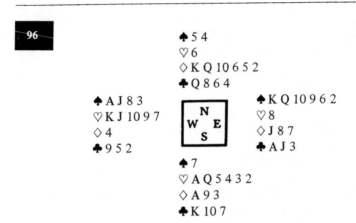

96

♠ 5 4
♥ 6
♦ K Q 10 6 5 2
♣ Q 8 6 4

♠ A J 8 3
♥ K J 10 9 7
♦ 4
♣ 9 5 2

♠ K Q 10 9 6 2
♥ 8
♦ J 8 7
♣ A J 3

♠ 7
♥ A Q 5 4 3 2
♦ A 9 3
♣ K 10 7

Only an unlikely club lead can defeat 4♠. In practice it would be made every time. Note that 5♦ by North-South is subject only to the club finesse.

97

North leads the ♦8. Declarer draws trumps and lays down the ♥AK. If both defenders follow he can claim, for he can set up his fifth heart by ruffing — twice if need be. The ♣AK provide the entries. Should hearts split 5-1 — less than a 15% chance — West will play South for the ♠A. If that, too, fails, the ♣Q may drop. It's long odds on the slam — especially if it is played from the right side.

98

Dlr. West
N/S Vul.

♠ 7 5 3 2
♡ —
◇ A K Q 9 8
♣ 8 6 4 2

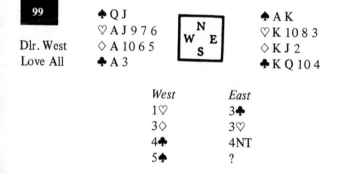

♠ K 9 4
♡ Q J 10 8 6
◇ 2
♣ A K 5 3

West	North	East	South
Pass	1♠	2♡	Dble
?			

No need to panic, still less to rescue. You have three tricks for partner, and that's more than he is entitled to expect. Conceivably, on the hand above, he would bid 3♣, but in any case, 2♡ should be superior to 3◇, which will surely be doubled.

99

Dlr. West
Love All

♠ Q J
♡ A J 9 7 6
◇ A 10 6 5
♣ A 3

♠ A K
♡ K 10 8 3
◇ K J 2
♣ K Q 10 4

West	East
1♡	3♣
3◇	3♡
4♣	4NT
5♠	?

If West has the ♡AQ East wants to be in a grand slam. Since, however, 4NT has been used to enquire about aces, 5NT would be an enquiry for kings, not the grand slam force. In such a situation, the bid of another suit replaces the *direct* 5NT. Hearts being the agreed suit, East bids 6◇ and, having only one of the top honours, West stops in 6♡.

98

South leads his ♠6 to North's ace. At trick two, he ruffs East's ♠K and exits with the ♣9. Declarer wins, cashes his second top club and continues with dummy's ◇AKQ, discarding two clubs. The lead of the ♣9 pinpointed the club position, so he knows that South has no more. Next, East ruffs a diamond.

> North: ♠AQJ108 ♡54 ◇J43 ♣QJ10
> South: ♠6 ♡AK9732 ◇10765 ♣97

Having scored six tricks, declarer exits with the ♣9, which South, with only trumps left, is obliged to ruff. Nothing can prevent East from making two more tricks for his contract.

In 3◇, perish the thought, West, without help from the defence, won't make more than seven tricks — the ◇AKQ, the ♣AK and two heart ruffs.

The time to rescue, and the only reason for doing it, is when you have a long suit, without tops, and no tricks for partner (as in **80**).

99

North leads the ♠10. This should have been a lay-down, but the duplication in spades, with 10 points yielding just two tricks, introduces an element of uncertainty. Declarer could lose a trump and a diamond. Can he ensure against such misfortune?

Unless North has a void in trumps, the answer is yes. West cashes his second spade, lays down the ♡A and leads the ♡J. If North follows, he finesses. Should South win, whatever he returns will enable West to dispose of his diamond loser. A club will allow for two diamond discards from the closed hand. A diamond will be tantamount to presenting declarer with a successful finesse. A spade will provide a ruff and discard.

Should North show out on the second heart, West will rise with dummy's ♡K and throw South in with a third heart. The result will be the same. In either case, having no more hearts, South will be helpless.

100

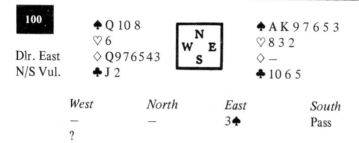

Dlr. East
N/S Vul.

West	North	East	South
—	—	3♠	Pass
?			

Opponents must surely have a slam, maybe a grand slam, and, since South passed, North is marked with a mighty hand. Would 4♠ shut him out? It's doubtful. Don't give him the chance to come in, perhaps with 4NT. Bid 5♠, a difficult hurdle for North to surmount, whatever his hand. Could partner misunderstand? Impossible. With slam ambitions West would cue-bid (as in **82**).

A frustrated North doubles and all pass.

101

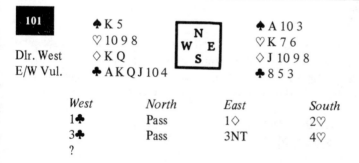

Dlr. West
E/W Vul.

West	North	East	South
1♣	Pass	1◇	2♡
3♣	Pass	3NT	4♡
?			

The chances of making ten tricks in no-trumps are problematical, but so are West's prospects in defence against 4♡. If both contracts are on, the swing could be huge. There's a case for a *forcing pass*, leaving East to decide. But can he be sure that the clubs are so solid? Surely not, so let's bid 4NT.

South leads the ◇K, North following with the ◇2, and suddenly what was intended as an advance sacrifice has become a makeable contract. North's ◇2 points to a 3-3 break, and if so, the diamonds can be set up, providing that declarer finds three entries in dummy — two to ruff diamonds in the closed hand, and another to get back to four established winners. This means that the finesse against the ♠J must succeed, so after ruffing the ◇K declarer leads a spade and inserts dummy's eight. If it holds, he is on the way to an unhoped-for victory.

> North: ♠ — ♡AK1097 ◇1082 ♣AKQ83
> South: ♠J42 ♡QJ54 ◇AKJ ♣974

Observe that North-South can make 7♡ or 7♣. The maximum swing, in duplicate terms, is 2860 and it would still be 2110 if only the small slam were bid. The moral? When you intend to shut out, go the whole hog. No half-measures.

South leads the ♡Q on which North throws the ◇3. East can see nine tricks, but where will the tenth come from? Looking ahead to a possible squeeze, he plays low. It's the right technique. South is bound to continue with hearts, since otherwise declarer would set up three diamonds.

> North: ♠Q9876 ♡ — ◇76543 ♣976
> South: ♠J42 ♡AQJ5432 ◇A2 ♣2

South continues with the ♡A and ♡J. East reels off dummy's clubs coming down to four cards. Dummy remains with ♠K5 ◇KQ facing ♠A103 ◇J. What has South kept? The ◇A and ...? If he is down to one heart, East can afford to set up a diamond. So South keeps ♠J ♡54 ◇A. The ♠K now fells the ♠J and East finesses confidently against North's ♠Q.

This is a *guard squeeze*, South having been forced to unguard his ♠J. Had East won the first trick the squeeze would not have materialised.

102

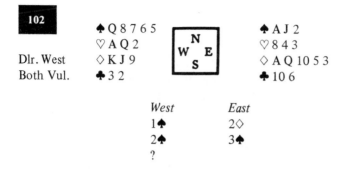

Dlr. West
Both Vul.

♠ Q 8 7 6 5
♡ A Q 2
◇ K J 9
♣ 3 2

♠ A J 2
♡ 8 4 3
◇ A Q 10 5 3
♣ 10 6

West	East
1♠	2◇
2♠	3♠
?	

You are not too proud of your spades and you have a minimum opening, so your first impulse is to pass. A moment's reflection, however,
and you see that your hand has greatly improved. Not only have the
diaphanous trumps solidified, but you have an excellent fit for partner's
suit. There must be a 50-50 chance for game, so you bid it.
    North doubles.

103

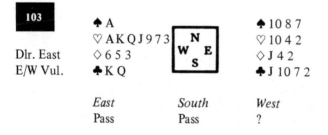

Dlr. East
E/W Vul.

♠ A
♡ A K Q J 9 7 3
◇ 6 5 3
♣ K Q

♠ 10 8 7
♡ 10 4 2
◇ J 4 2
♣ J 10 7 2

East	South	West
Pass	Pass	?

With nine playing tricks, this qualifies for a 2♡ bid − or 1♣ or 2♣,
according the system. By any standard you're much too good for a
pre-emptive 4♡, yet that is precisely the iconoclasm I advocate at this
vulnerability in third position. Should you miss a slam it will be entirely
your fault, but it's much more likely that you will prevent opponents
from finding a cheap save − or even a lucky make.

102

North begins with the two top clubs and switches to a diamond. Left to yourself you would finesse the ♠J, hoping to find North with a doubleton ♠K. The double transforms the situation. North must have four trumps, perhaps ♠K109x. So you begin with the ♠Q. With any luck you might pin South's ♠9 or ♠10. But it's not to be.

North: ♠K1093 ♡KJ5 ◇762 ♣AK7
South: ♠4 ♡10976 ◇84 ♣QJ9854

North covers and the ♠A wins. Back with a diamond you lead the ♠8. Again North covers and the ♠J takes a trick. A third spade is won by North, but whatever he returns, declarer draws his last trump and claims.

Without the tell-tale double the contract could never have been made. And such is often the case. A greedy double may bring in an extra 100 — or cost 800 or so.

103

North leads the ♠K, on which South plays the ♠9. You've certainly missed nothing, but can you make 4♡?

Your best chance is to play the ♣K at once. If South wins and returns a spade, you'll have time to discard two diamonds on dummy's ♣J10, the ♡10 being the entry. Should you draw even one round of trumps and find North with a void, he'll probably signal in diamonds. South's ♠9 will have told him that he started with two or four and your pre-emptive 4♡ makes it quite likely that the ♠A was bare.

North: ♠KQ432 ♡ — ◇AQ108 ♣9653
South: ♠J965 ♡865 ◇K97 ♣A84

Yes, North could have the ♣A, but if so he may not like to play away from a tenace, the ◇AQ or K10. Perhaps he should do, but putting defenders to a guess is your best chance. Even the best defenders don't always guess right.

104

♠ Q 10 8
♡ K Q 10 6 5
Dlr. West   ◇ K Q 2
Both Vul.   ♣ A Q

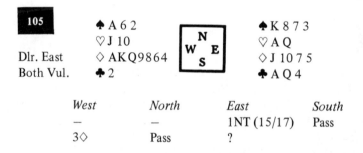

♠ 6 5 2
♡ A J 7
◇ A 5 4 3
♣ 10 7 6

West	East
1♡	1NT
2NT	?

Two aces are worth more than 8 points any day, so there can be no question of passing, but should East make the book bid of 3♡ – forcing, of course – or should he settle for the cheaper contract of 3NT? With no ruffing value, I confess that I prefer 3NT. East, however, makes the 'correct' bid of 3♡ and West calls the game in hearts.

105

♠ A 6 2
♡ J 10
Dlr. East   ◇ A K Q 9 8 6 4
Both Vul.   ♣ 2

♠ K 8 7 3
♡ A Q
◇ J 10 7 5
♣ A Q 4

West	North	East	South
–	–	1NT (15/17)	Pass
3◇	Pass	?	

A jump to 3♡ or 3♠ over 1NT suggests game in the major in preference to no-trumps. A jump in a minor invites a slam. Without such ambitions, responder would bid 3NT, occasionally 5◇ (or 5♣). Accepting the invitation, East makes the cheapest available cue-bid, 3♡, then, over 3♠, he shows the ♣A. Let's say that South doubles. There can't be enough for a grand slam, so West settles for 6◇.

104

North leads the ♠4 to South's ♠A. The ♠J comes back. You cover, North wins with the ♠K and returns the ♠3, ruffed by South, who plays back the ♣4.

Left to yourself, you would draw trumps and test the diamonds, falling back on the club finesse, if they didn't break. Now, you can't try both — you must choose. The finesse is a 50-50 chance; the 3-3 break is only one chance in three.

Don't finesse. Pay heed to North's return of the ♠3, his lowest. With no reason to deceive anyone he is signalling for a club. Without preference he would return the ♠7.

> North: ♠K9743 ♡98 ◇J1076 ♣K8
> South: ♠AJ ♡432 ◇98 ♣J95432

The diamonds are 4-2 but North has the length, and on your last heart, coming down to four cards, he must shed a precious diamond or the ♣K.

105

In response to South's double, North leads the ♣9. West has eleven top tricks. The ♣K is obviously offside, but he has two other chances, the heart finesse or a 3-3 spade break. By testing the latter first, he can combine the two. Good odds, yet they can be improved considerably through *partial elimination*.

Having drawn trumps, West ruffs dummy's ♣4, cashes the ♠A and ♠K, and leads the ♣Q, throwing his third spade on South's ♣K. A heart or club back would be immediately fatal. If South returns a spade, West will ruff, and if the suit doesn't break 3-3, he will still have the heart finesse available. But he will have another chance, too, that if the spades are 4-2, North, not South, will have the long spade.

> North: ♠J1054 ♡97432 ◇2 ♣985
> South: ♠Q9 ♡K865 ◇3 ♣KJ10763

106

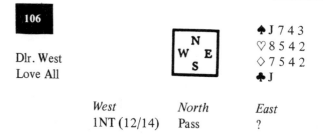

Dlr. West
Love All

♠ J 7 4 3
♡ 8 5 4 2
◇ 7 5 4 2
♣ J

West	North	East
1NT (12/14)	Pass	?

One thing is certain. If East passes, South will have enough to double, North will be only too happy to pass and there will be a steep price to pay. An escape into any one of three suits would save a lot of points. Even 2◇ on a 4-3 fit would be better and a double isn't certain. Seek refuge in Stayman.

Alas, there's no 4-4 fit. West bids 2◇.

107

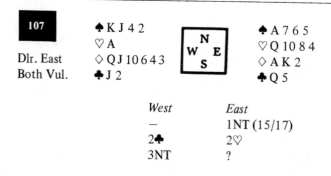

♠ K J 4 2
♡ A
◇ Q J 10 6 4 3
♣ J 2

♠ A 7 6 5
♡ Q 10 8 4
◇ A K 2
♣ Q 5

Dlr. East
Both Vul.

West	East
—	1NT (15/17)
2♣	2♡
3NT	?

Since partner has no fit in hearts he must have four spades and, though there should be more than enough for 3NT, there's no need to run any risks. Bid 4♠.

With both majors, which one should opener show first? The inferences being inescapable, it doesn't matter. There's no unanimity among experts.

106

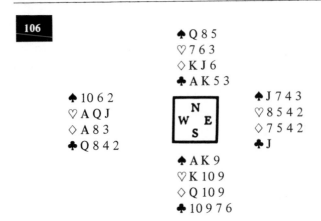

```
                    ♠ Q 8 5
                    ♡ 7 6 3
                    ◇ K J 6
                    ♣ A K 5 3
    ♠ 10 6 2        ┌─────────┐        ♠ J 7 4 3
    ♡ A Q J         │    N    │        ♡ 8 5 4 2
    ◇ A 8 3       W │         │ E      ◇ 7 5 4 2
    ♣ Q 8 4 2       │    S    │        ♣ J
                    └─────────┘
                    ♠ A K 9
                    ♡ K 10 9
                    ◇ Q 10 9
                    ♣ 10 9 7 6
```

The distribution being favourable, West should make six tricks, though even five would show a profit over 1NT doubled. Of course, North-South may not double 2◇, but can they bid or make 3NT?

107

South leads out the ♣AK and switches to a diamond. Which East-West cards should make up the next trick?

Declarer faces dangers on two fronts — a diamond ruff and a 4-1 trump break, and he must guard against both. The first threat compels him to start with the two top trumps, without attempting a finesse, for if North has the doubleton ♠Q he could give South a ruff. The second threat dictates the order of play in the trump suit, a spade to the ♠K, then the ♠A. Should North show out, a third spade, up to the ♠J, will leave South on play with the ♠Q. Whatever he returns, West will draw the last trump and take the rest.

If North has the queen to four trumps there's no remedy.

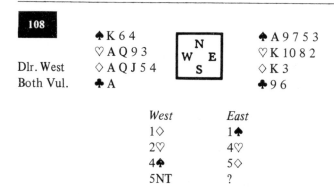

108		

♠ K 6 4   ♠ A 9 7 5 3
♡ A Q 9 3   ♡ K 10 8 2
Dlr. West   ◇ A Q J 5 4   ◇ K 3
Both Vul.   ♣ A   ♣ 9 6

West	East
1◇	1♠
2♡	4♡
4♠	5◇
5NT	?

Ostensibly, West's 5NT, the grand slam force, seeks two of the three top honours in hearts. In fact, he only wants to make sure of the ♡K. East makes the standard reply, 6♣, showing a top and four hearts (see **7**). What of the ♠A? It's an inference, but without it, East wouldn't have cue-bid 5◇.

109		

♠ A 9 8 6 4   ♠ K Q J 10 7 5
Dlr. South   ♡ A K 9   ♡ J 10 6
Both Vul.   ◇ Q 9 5   ◇ 7 4 2
E/W 30   ♣ A Q   ♣ J
Rubber Bridge

South	West	North	East
Pass	1♠	Pass	4♠
Pass	?		

If East has a good hand, West's 19 points and three first round controls justify high ambitions. East, however, *cannot* have a good hand. He bid over the score not to spur West on to better things, but to shut out opponents. It must be so, for if he had slam aspirations, he would have bid another suit or maybe 3NT, certainly not 4♠. So West passes.

108

North leads the ♣K against 7♡. Subject to the likely 3-2 trump break, the grand slam is cold. Three spades from dummy are discarded on the diamonds and a spade ruff provides the thirteenth trick.

> North: ♠QJ10 ♡75 ◇10876 ♣KQ32
> South: ♠82 ♡J64 ◇92 ♣J108754

Note that with diamonds as trumps there would only be twelve tricks and it would be the same if dummy had three or even four diamonds, say: ♠A97 ♡K1082 ◇K1098 ♣96.

Paradoxically, when both hands have four cards in the same suit and five facing four in another, the eight cards divided 4-4 yield more tricks as trumps than nine split 5-4. This is because the unevenly divided suit allows a discard from a side-suit, which, in turn, creates an extra trick by ruffing, as above.

109

North leads the ◇3 to South's ◇K. On the ◇A, which follows, he throws a club. He ruffs a third diamond and exits with a trump. Now it's South who throws a club.

Three tricks have been lost and there's a question mark over the hearts. Should declarer take the heart finesse or the club finesse, or maybe cash the ♡AK and if the ♡Q doesn't drop, take the finesse in clubs?

All three are destined to fail. South has shown a good 6-card suit and a shapely hand. With either the ♡Q or the ♣K he wouldn't have passed. He did, so North must have both these cards. Playing accordingly, West cashes the ♡AK and plays out the trumps, throwing a heart on the last one. Dummy's remaining two cards are: ♡J ♣J facing the ♣AQ. If North still has the ♡Q his ♣K will drop.

110

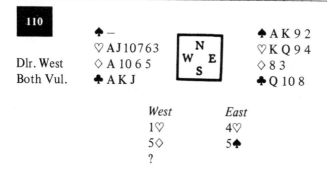

♠ —
♡ A J 10 7 6 3
♢ A 10 6 5
♣ A K J

Dlr. West
Both Vul.

♠ A K 9 2
♡ K Q 9 4
♢ 8 3
♣ Q 10 8

West	East
1♡	4♡
5♢	5♠
?	

West could apply the grand slam force with 5NT, calling on East to bid 7♡ with two of the three top honours, but that wouldn't be enough to ensure thirteen tricks. The bidding can no longer stop short of 6♡, so any other bid suggests a grand slam. Has East anything to spare? West puts the question: 6♣. With more than enough for his raise to 4♡, East accepts the invitation and bids 7♡.

111

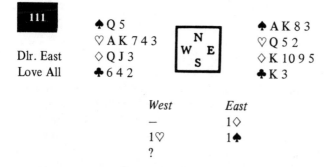

♠ Q 5
♡ A K 7 4 3
♢ Q J 3
♣ 6 4 2

Dlr. East
Love All

♠ A K 8 3
♡ Q 5 2
♢ K 10 9 5
♣ K 3

West	East
—	1♢
1♡	1♠
?	

The modern practice would be to call 2♣. The fourth suit is forcing and asks partner for further information. Here he can pick between 2♡, too timid, 3♡, which is best, and 2NT, indicating a stopper in clubs. West, however, chose an old-fashioned 2NT, and East, who should have bid 3♡ in case West had a 5-card suit, raised to 3NT, obviously an inferior contract to 4♡.

110

North leads a trump.

I don't blame either party, but the tiresome duplication makes the grand slam a non-starter — or so it would appear. West has, however, one advantage. No one knows of his void in spades, so each defender, in turn, will be anxious to guard the suit.

> North: ♠Q10763 ♡82 ◇KJ7 ♣973
> South: ♠J854 ♡5 ◇Q942 ♣6542

Smoothly West reels off nine winners — six hearts and the ♣AKQ, leaving himself with ◇A1065 and dummy with ♠AK9 ◇8. Which will be the last four cards in defenders' hands?

Assuming that West *must* have a spade, if not two — why else didn't he play off the ♠AK when he was in dummy? — North and South will both cling to three spades and so, perforce, bare their diamonds honours. The spade mirage will have promoted the ◇1065 into tricks.

111

North leads the ♠J. Assuming the likely 3-2 break in hearts, you have eight tricks. Where should you look for the ninth?

If South has the ◇A he can do no harm, and if North has the ♣A, all is well anyway. So your sole concern should be with finding the aces reversed. Can you still make 3NT? Not against the best defence and that is when you should look for the second best. Winning the first trick in hand you should try to slip through the ◇J. Not every North will go up every time with the ◇A, if he has it, to shoot through a club. And if he doesn't, you'll have your ninth trick and concentrate on the other eight.

It's an elementary piece of deception, but succeeds surprisingly often, especially if declarer plays quickly and smoothly. North could have: ♠J1097 ♡1086 ◇A42 ♣Q95.

112

	♠ 8 5 3 2		♠ —
	♡ A 7 6 4		♡ 9 8
Dlr. West	◇ K 9		◇ A J 10 8 7 4
E/W Vul.	♣ A 6 2		♣ K Q J 8 4

West	North	East	South
Pass	1♡	2NT	Pass
3♡	3♠	4♠	Pass
?			

The *unusual* 2NT, bid directly over one in a major, shows eleven cards, occasionally ten, in the minors. This convention, like so many others, readily lends itself to abuse and players captivated by their shape, are apt to bid on inadequate values. Here, the adverse vulnerability precludes liberties. The cue-bid in spades is just what he wants to hear, and with two invaluable cards in the minors, West calls 6♣.

113

	♠ 10 9 7 6		♠ A K Q J 8 5
	♡ K 7 6 5 4		♡ A J 9 3 2
Dlr. West	◇ K Q		◇ —
N/S Vul.	♣ A Q		♣ J 3

West	East
1♡	2♠
3♠	4♡
5♣	5NT
6◇	?

West's 6◇ shows one of the two top honours and five hearts (see **7**), so the ♡Q is likely to drop. The spades are solid. Which suit, then, should be trumps? Hearts, because they are *evenly divided*. Just as 4-4 in trumps with 5-4 in a side suit is superior to a 5-4 trump fit, so 5-5 is superior to 6-5 or 6-4. The same principle applies as in **108**. Bid 7♡.

112

North leads the ♠K, ruffed in dummy. West plays the ♣A and ♣K, both defenders following. A heart loser being inevitable, all hinges on the diamonds.

It's easy enough, so long as declarer is in the habit of card-reading, visualising opponents' hands in the light of the bidding and early play. North, who opened 1♡, wouldn't bid 3♠ on a 4-card suit, so he must have five. And he followed twice in clubs. That leaves no room for a diamond.

> North: ♠AKQJ9 ♡KQ10532 ◇ — ♣109
> South: ♠10764 ♡J ◇Q6532 ♣753

Should West, doing 'what comes naturally', draw the last trump, he can never recover.

After the second round of trumps, however, he finesses the ◇9, which must win. Next he overtakes the ◇K with the ◇A and takes a ruffing finesse against the ◇Q — which is why he needed his third trump. South is helpless.

113

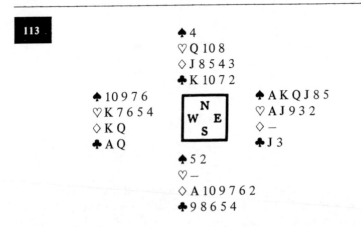

♠ 4
♡ Q 10 8
◇ J 8 5 4 3
♣ K 10 7 2

♠ 10 9 7 6   ♠ A K Q J 8 5
♡ K 7 6 5 4   ♡ A J 9 3 2
◇ K Q   ◇ —
♣ A Q   ♣ J 3

♠ 5 2
♡ —
◇ A 10 9 7 6 2
♣ 9 8 6 5 4

West ruffs the opening diamond, draws trumps, cashes the ♣A and discards his ♣Q on a long spade. A club ruff is his thirteenth trick. With spades as trumps there are only twelve.

114

Dlr. South
Love All

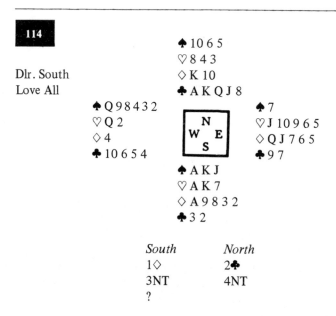

```
                    ♠ 10 6 5
                    ♡ 8 4 3
                    ◇ K 10
                    ♣ A K Q J 8
♠ Q 9 8 4 3 2                        ♠ 7
♡ Q 2              ┌─────────┐       ♡ J 10 9 6 5
◇ 4               │   N     │       ◇ Q J 7 6 5
♣ 10 6 5 4        │ W   E   │       ♣ 9 7
                   │   S     │
                   └─────────┘
                    ♠ A K J
                    ♡ A K 7
                    ◇ A 9 8 3 2
                    ♣ 3 2
```

South	North
1◇	2♣
3NT	4NT
?	

Should South bid 6NT? He has enough, but he can do better by bidding 5◇. Like North's 4NT, this has nothing to do with Blackwood. It simply shows a 5-card suit, in case North has a fit. Having none, he signs off in 5♡. Again, this is no convention, just the cheapest way to deny support for a slam in diamonds. South settles for 6NT.

This is how these hands were bid by the Frenchmen, Faigenbaum and Stetten, in a match against Italy.

A club was led. South took the losing spade finesse, won the club return and cashed all but one of his winners — the ♠AK, the ♡AK, the ◇K and three clubs. The last one left dummy with the ♡8 ◇10, facing ◇A98. West had only spades left. Declarer had a count on his hand as soon as East showed out in the black suits. In the 2-card ending, East was forced to give up his master heart or to bare the ◇Q. Either way South had his twelfth trick.

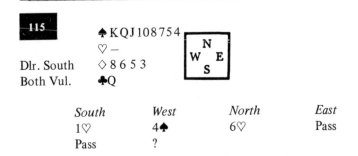

115	♠KQJ108754			
	♡ –			
Dlr. South	◇8653			
Both Vul.	♣Q			

South	West	North	East
1♡	4♠	6♡	Pass
Pass	?		

When pre-empts raise the bidding to the six level on the first round there are no charts or tables to consult. No rules apply. A player must draw such inferences as are available and rely on his judgment.

Clearly, North has an exotic distribution and a void – no doubt in spades – since he didn't invoke Blackwood. How about East? With two likely tricks in defence he would have doubled, not so much to inflict a penalty, as to warn West against sacrificing. Since he hasn't doubled, he must have one defensive trick or none.

If North-South make their slam they will score 1430, so even going four down – five down at matchpoint scoring – will show a profit. With no defence – the ♣Q is hardly worth considering – West should have no hesitation in bidding 6♠.

115

♠ K Q J 10 8 7 5 4   ♠ 9 6
♡ —   ♡ 6 4 2
◇ 8 6 5 3   ◇ A Q 10 7
♣ Q   ♣ 7 5 4 2

North leads the ♡A. West ruffs and plays the ♠K on which North throws the ◇2. South rises with the ♠A and plays the ♣6. The ♣Q wins!

Is South mad? No? Why, then, has he underled the ♣AK?

Clearly he hopes to find partner with ♣QJ or Q10 and ruff diamonds twice, thus collecting an 1100 penalty instead of a mere 500. Against the slender risk of finding the existing distribution, he sees the alluring prospect of an extra 600. To take advantage of this unexpected windfall West draws trumps and plays the ◇8, ready to run it unless North covers. He does, so West inserts the ◇10 which wins.

North: ♠ — ♡AKQ8 ◇KJ942 ♣J1093
South: ♠A32 ♡J109753 ◇ — ♣AK86

Back with a club ruff, declarer leads another diamond, covers North's ◇J with the ◇Q and repeats the process to make a contract for which he was prepared to pay 1100 as a sacrifice.

I have introduced this hand not just as an unexpectedly happy ending, but because it carries a message. Perfect contracts may run up against unerring defence and unlucky breaks. But the reverse happens, too. A defender takes 'a wrong view', as above, and the distribution allows a seemingly impossible contract to be brought home. The moral is that a player should be as ready to make the most of his luck as he is to guard against misfortune.

There is a tide in the affairs of man which, taken at the flood, leads on to fortune.